Practical Payroll

How to administer Pay As You Earn, National Insurance, Statutory Sick Pay and Statutory Maternity Pay

Written by:

Stuart Howard BA (Hons)
Keith Kirkland MSc BSc

Published by:
Vector Business Development
Vector House
Springles Lane
Titchfield
Hampshire PO15 6RR

Tel: 01329 845693
Fax: 01329 843743

ISBN 1 900350 01 7

Although the authors believe the contents to be accurate and correct, and all possible care has been taken to produce this work, no guarantee can be given. You should take proper advice prior to making any decisions. This work should provide you with good background information however.

Illustrations by John Loader

PP/09/1997

Contents

Introduction

We hope that this workbook will make life easier for people learning how to calculate wages and salaries. You will realise just how much there is to learn if you look at the Inland Revenue and Department of Social Security reference manuals!

We have taken the content of these manuals, simplified it, attempted to put it into a logical order for new starters and added topics not covered in the 'official' manuals like payroll law, pension schemes and payment methods and procedures.

You will need to be familiar with the various government forms, manuals and tables. If you have problems getting hold of these, don't worry. Providing you have access to a personal computer, you can look up the manuals on the Practical Payroll CD. We gratefully acknowledge the help provided by the Inland Revenue in producing the CD. If, despite our considerable efforts, you find any errors or omissions, you can be sure the mistakes are ours not theirs!

All our illustrations are based on manual payroll calculations using government forms and guides. This doesn't mean that we dislike computerised payroll programmes - far from it! However, you *must* be able to calculate taxes manually if you are to understand, and update, your computerised payroll programme. Who knows, you may even find a bug in your payroll programme!

Payroll staff often receive little or no training. This is surprising, bearing in mind that labour is the biggest item of expenditure for many businesses. Income tax and national insurance calculations are plagued with complications and exceptions. It is easy to make mistakes, some of which are punishable by fines. This is galling to businesses who never volunteered to act as unpaid tax collectors in the first place. Nor do they like acting as unpaid administrators for government sick pay or maternity schemes!

Self assessment has made the payroll administrator's job even more important. Your business now has to meet strict guidelines for the supply of information to the firm's employees and to the Inland Revenue. If these guidelines are breached, the business faces automatic penalties.

In smaller firms, the person who administers the payroll may find themselves responsible for other pay related activities like pensions, holiday administration, beneficial loans, luncheon vouchers, expenses and employment records. We will look at some of these related activities as we work our way through the book.

Purpose of this Workbook

This workbook will introduce:

- Pay As You Earn (PAYE)
- National Insurance Contributions
- Statutory Sick Pay
- Statutory Maternity Pay.

Here are some brief introductory notes on each topic.

Pay As You Earn (PAYE)

Pay As You Earn is a system of collecting income tax from employed people. In theory, income is only taxable if it meets specific criteria. In practice, the criteria are so widely drawn that it is almost impossible to escape the taxman. The rules of taxation are laid down in Acts of Parliament. Different kinds of income are collected under different rules (or 'schedules' as they are called).

As a matter of interest, the income tax schedules are listed below together with the kinds of income they apply to:

Schedule A	Rents from land and unfurnished lettings
Schedule C	Certain types of interest taxed at source
Schedule D	Profits from trade and some investment income
Schedule E	Income from employment
Schedule F	Dividends from companies.

Notice that there is no Schedule B - this was originally a tax on woodlands. Schedule B was abolished in 1988 (woodlands are now taxed under Schedule D).

We are only concerned in this workbook with the rules of Schedule E - which is income from wages, salaries, commissions, bonuses etc. Schedule E applies to all *employed* persons. Schedule E income tax is collected by a procedure known as Pay As You Earn (PAYE). PAYE enables the Inland Revenue to collect tax at regular intervals, usually weekly or monthly. Income tax is administered by the Inland Revenue.

The Inland Revenue is divided into two main branches:

(i) The Inspector of Taxes
(ii) The Collector of Taxes.

The Inspectors decide how much tax you have to pay. The Collectors are responsible for collecting the money. This division of responsibility is common to many other organisations. It is designed to minimise the possibility of fraud and collusion.

If you have queries about the *amount* of tax which has to be collected, you will liaise with your local inspector. If you have queries concerning payment of money, you need to talk to the Collector of Taxes. If you regard them as two totally separate organisations, you can't go far wrong.

Income tax is covered in Sections 2 to 11 of this book.

National Insurance

National Insurance is the second form of taxation we will be exploring in this workbook. National Insurance was introduced in the National Insurance Act of 1946. This act brought about the introduction of the modern welfare system as we know it. Originally national insurance was devised as a means of paying for the welfare state. Now all tax receipts are added together with no particular tax being earmarked for any particular purpose.

Like income tax, national insurance is also a tax on wages and salaries. National insurance is levied on ***gross*** income which seems a little unfair since part of your income is normally taken away by income tax!

All employees with a satisfactory national insurance contributions record are entitled to a range of state welfare benefits and a basic state pension. The more you earn, the higher the rate of tax that you pay. In the jargon, these taxes are called 'graduated contributions'.

National insurance is administered by the Department of Social Security. If you have any queries about national insurance payments, you can resolve these with your local national insurance office. Be aware that not every national insurance office deals with client queries, some addresses in the telephone directory are Department of Social Security buildings devoted purely to their internal administration.

National insurance is introduced in Section 12 of this book.

Statutory Sick Pay

Statutory Sick Pay (SSP) is a government scheme which requires employers to pay wages to employees who are unfit for work because of illness. The Department of Social Security is responsible for the administration of SSP. Like all government schemes, the operation of statutory sick pay is governed by strict rules. We will look at these rules in more detail in Section 13. For the purposes of this brief introduction, we will simply say that people who have been ill for more than three days qualify for statutory sick pay. SSP is operated and paid for by the employer. Under certain circumstances, the employer may be able to recover part of the SSP from the government. These recoveries are made by deducting cash from the employees' income tax and national insurance contributions which are normally paid over to the government each month. The government sets the minimum amount of SSP but the employer is free to 'top this up' to whatever level is deemed appropriate. You may be surprised to learn that SSP is subject to tax.

Statutory Maternity Pay

Statutory Maternity Pay (SMP) is another government scheme which is administered by the employer. Employees who become pregnant are entitled to statutory maternity pay providing they meet certain conditions. We will examine statutory maternity pay in more detail in Section 14. For the moment, however, we will simply say that, in broad outline, women are entitled to be paid for up to 18 weeks maternity leave provided that they have worked for their current employer for at least 26 weeks. They must also be able to supply medical evidence from their doctor to prove that they are pregnant. The employee can choose which weeks best suit her maternity needs. Statutory maternity pay is only payable provided that the employee does not work; ladies cannot earn wages and draw SMP at the same time. The employer is entitled to recover all, or nearly all, of the SMP paid to employees. The employer's SMP reimbursement is taken from the tax and national insurance monies collected by the business. Employers can 'top up' the ladies' earnings during pregnancy leave should they choose to do so. SMP is taxable. The Department of Social Security is the government department responsible for SMP.

Scope of the Workbook

Government legislation has created complicated rules concerning pay, benefits, expenses, social security payments, tax, pensions etc. The purpose of this workbook is to introduce some of these regulations and link the information available from a variety of government publications. Where possible, the source of reference information is given. This will enable you to follow up the content in more detail if you need to do so.

Don't forget to make use of the employers' help lines if you get stuck with employees' payroll problems. For general enquiries, you can call 0345-143-143. This offers help on Inland Revenue and Contributions Agency problems. Alternatively, you can call your local Social Security office or PAYE tax office for more specific advice relevant to your business. The Inland Revenue and Contributions Agency run free workshops and seminars which help people learning to calculate wages.

The Workbook Characters

Throughout the workbook, we have used a set of imaginary characters to illustrate how Pay As You Earn and National Insurance work. These characters are introduced on the next page. They all work for a rural brewery called Mainbrew.

Meet Mainbrew's Employees

Bill Gates

Bill helps produce the beer which Mainbrew sells. We will see how:

- he is taxed under PAYE
- we handle his P45 form when he leaves Mainbrew and joins rival Technobrew.

Sally from Sales

Sally is the sales representative for Mainbrew. She earns over £8,500 per annum and has a company car. We will see how she is taxed on the private use of her company car. We will also see how her other expenses and benefits are assessed.

Wendie from Wages

Wendie is the payroll administrator for Mainbrew. We will see how she handles:

- Wages and National Insurance Contributions
- Year end reporting to the tax authorities
- Statutory Sick Pay
- Statutory Maternity Pay.

Malcolm the MD

Malcolm is a director of Mainbrew Ltd. We will see how he is taxed on his:

- Expenses and Benefits
- Annual Performance Bonus
- National Insurance Contributions
- Company Pension.

Bill

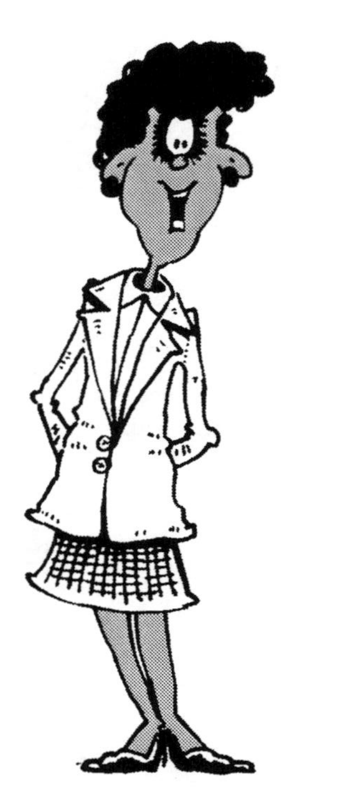

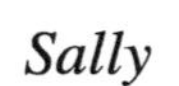

Sally

Wendie

Malcolm

What is an Employee?

Normally, of course, it is easy to decide whether a person working for you is employed or self employed. The distinction is important because the Inland Revenue and the Department of Social Security (DSS) treat employed and self employed people in a completely different way.

To make matters even more complicated, *you* could decide that your work is being performed by a self employed person, whereas the Inland Revenue and DSS may classify that worker as your employee. In an extreme case, this could lead to you, the employer, paying tax which should be borne by the self employed person.

It is important to be clear about a worker's employment status because this will affect:

- whether they are taxed under the rules of Schedule E or Schedule D
- whether Class 1 and Class 1A National Insurance Contributions apply
- whether they are entitled to sick pay (SSP) and, possibly, maternity pay (SMP)
- whether they are entitled to join a company pension scheme
- whether they need a Contract of Employment
- whether they are entitled to employment protection, eg unfair dismissal and redundancy payments
- whether they are entitled to holiday pay

etc.

Fortunately, both DSS and the Inland Revenue work to the same guidelines. This means that once one department has reached a decision on a worker's status then this will normally be accepted by the other department. You need to be clear about the distinction between employment and self employment. Guidance is given in booklet IR56/NI39, 'Employed or Self Employed?' available either from your local Contributions Agency or Inland Revenue Enquiries Office. Both bodies employ officers who can be consulted on employment status. Also have a look at page 6 of the Employer's Further Guide to PAYE and NICs, CWG2 (1997).

Employed or self employed?

Employed Persons

In general, employees:

- have a Contract of Employment
- are paid by the hour, week or month
- are often entitled to overtime pay
- tend to work set hours, eg so many hours per week or month
- work at their employer's premises or at other locations decided by the employer
- are told what to do, when to do it and, sometimes, how to do their work (the Inland Revenue call this a master/servant relationship)
- do not have to find someone else to do their job if they are absent.

It is the ***employer's*** responsibility by law to collect tax from employed persons. This taxation takes the form of:

- PAYE income tax which is administered by the Inland Revenue, and
- Class 1 (and Class 1A) National Insurance Contributions which are administered by the Contributions Agency which belongs to the Department of Social Security.

We have said that it is the employer's responsibility to calculate PAYE and NI deductions and pay them to the government. However, the employer is entitled to recover the tax from the employee's pay. If, for any reason, the deductions cannot be recovered from the employee then the employer may have to pay the tax himself.

Self Employed Persons

In general, self employed people:

- decide how the work is to be done
- provide their own tools and equipment to perform the work
- risk their own money in performing their work
- have to suffer the losses as well as take the profits
- can send substitute workers if they choose to
- have to repair unsatisfactory work at their own expense.

Self employed persons are responsibe for paying tax themselves. They pay:

- Income tax to the Inland Revenue under the rules of Schedule D
- Class 2 and Class 4 National Insurance Contributions to the Contributions Agency.

Although self employed persons are normally responsible for paying their own tax, the building industry is an exception. The main building contractor is required to deduct basic rate tax from the labour element of monies paid to self employed construction workers. The sub contractors then have to claim back excess amounts of tax collected under this system. The sub contractor can avoid having tax deducted by the main contractor if he applies for exemption via a '714 Certificate' (see IR14/15 Construction Industry Tax Deduction Scheme). If a sub contractor works for a continuous period for one main contractor, he may be classified as an employee by the Inland Revenue.

This book only looks at taxation of employed people, self employed taxation is dealt with in another book in this series called 'Taxation'.

Special Types of Employee

Pay As You Earn and Class 1 National Insurance are broad based taxes which affect most employed persons in a similar way. However, special rules apply to the types of employment listed below. The Employer's Further Guide to PAYE and NICs, booklet CWG2 (1997) tells you how to handle these cases.

- Divers
- Students
- Employees involved in a trade dispute or lock out
- Young persons on a Youth Training Scheme
- Gang Squad and Butty Systems - people who work them
- Employees who come from abroad
- Employees who are sent abroad
- Agency workers
- Casual workers
- Merchant seamen (they have different NIC regulations)
- Married women entitled to pay reduced rate NICs
- Company directors.

Divers are a special case

What is Pay?

Many people think of pay as simply the wage or salary earned from employment. However, from a taxation viewpoint, this is quite wrong. Pay not only includes money, it also includes any form of benefit which has a value, eg company car, interest free loan, home telephone bill paid etc. Pay, therefore, breaks down into two elements:

- Wages and salaries paid to employees each week or month
- Benefits and certain kinds of expense payments.

It is important to understand both elements of pay. Let's have a look at them in a little more detail.

Wages and Salaries

Most forms of pay are taxable. Here are some examples, the list is not exhaustive.

- Wages, salaries, fees, bonus and overtime
- Pensions
- Statutory Sick Pay
- Statutory Maternity Pay
- Vouchers or credit tokens
- Tips or service charges given to the employee
- Payments for travel time and travelling expenses between home and work
- Christmas bonuses
- Cash payments for meals at the normal place of work
- Cash awards for exceptional performances.

Benefits and Expense Payments

Benefits and expenses are generally taxable for:

- Directors, and
- Employees who earn more than £8,500 per annum (including the value of the benefits).

Benefits are so important that the whole of Section 9 is devoted to it later in the book. For the moment, however, let's have a look at some simple examples of benefits which count towards 'pay' for directors and employees earning more than £8,500.

Entertaining is taxable!

- Private use of company cars
- Private medical or dental treatment
- Private telephone rental and cost of calls (including mobile phones)
- Loans at attractive interest rates
- Employers paying off private credit card debts
- Goods or services provided at less than their full cost.

This list is not exhaustive. Pages 75 to 77 of the Employer's Further Guide to PAYE and NICs, CWG2 (1997) offers a more comprehensive listing.

Although ***all*** directors and those earning more than £8,500 (including the value of the benefits) are taxed on the value of the benefits, individuals earning less than £8,500 (including the value of the benefits) do not have to pay tax on those benefits.

What isn't Pay

Some benefits don't count towards taxable income. These exceptions include:

- Canteen meals provided for staff generally
- Meal vouchers worth 15p per day or less
- Car parking facilities at or near an employee's place of work
- Employees' contributions to a pension scheme.

Need More Information?

The following special cases of payment are covered in the Employer's Further Guide to PAYE and NICs, CWG2 (1997). The figures in brackets refer to page numbers.

- Prize incentive schemes (23)
- Holiday Pay (24)
- Tips and service charges (28)
- Training courses (72)
- Transport vouchers (72)
- Travel and subsistence payments (81)
- Scholarship apprentice and training schemes (77)
- Personal incidental expenses (71)
- Round sum allowances (81)
- Restrictive covenant payments (89)
- Profit related pay (91)
- Payroll giving schemes (22)
- Lump sum payments (87-90).

Holiday Pay is taxable

Payroll and the Law

Life would be wonderful if all the legislation affecting payroll was collected together and updated every year. The payroll administrator would then have a single clear reference work to go by. Unfortunately, life isn't like that. We are controlled by English and Scottish laws but these are modified by decisions made by the European Union. It is very hard to keep up to date in all the areas of law which could affect payroll. Big corporations can afford to employ specialists to keep their company up to date. However, the vast majority of businesses in Britain only employ a few people (96% of businesses in Britain employ 20 or less). You may find the following notes useful if you don't have a legal department or a human resources department on hand to dispense advice.

The Finance Acts

The employer is required by law to deduct income tax and national insurance from employees' wages. The legislation governing this is the Finance Act which is amended each year in the budget. Normally the budget is announced in November and implemented in the following April. This gives the Civil Service time to produce the revised tables and instructions for the new tax year. These revised instructions are usually distributed in February and March.

The Finance Acts also require businesses to make certain returns by law. These include:

- A quarterly report of any changes in company vehicles, form P46(Car), made available to employees for private use (see Section 9)
- Annual returns for taxes collected from employees' wages (see Section 8)
- Annual reports on benefits given to workers (see Section 9).

Employment Law

Most employment law is based on the Employment Protection (Consolidation) Act 1978. Amongst other things, this act requires the employer to give every employee a Contract of Employment. The Contract of Employment is very important from a payroll point of view. It stipulates pay and benefits entitlement for all new employees. It also lists the rules relating to sickness and sickness pay, holiday entitlement and holiday pay, and the intervals at which wages are paid.

Here are some notes on the Contract of Employment.

Contract of Employment

The Contract of Employment should covers the following headings. Items shown in *italics* (on the next page) are only required by businesses which have 20 employees or more.

- The names of the employer and the employee.
- The date when the employment began.
- The date when the employee's period of continuous employment began.
- The rate of pay or the method of calculating a week's pay.
- The intervals at which wages are paid.
- The terms and conditions relating to hours of work.
- The terms and conditions that relate to holiday entitlement, including information dealing with accrued holiday pay, holiday entitlement, and holiday pay on the termination of their employment.
- The terms and conditions relating to incapacity for work due to sickness or injury, the employer must also identify any provision for sickness pay.
- The terms and conditions that apply to pensions and pension schemes.
- The length of notice which the employee is required to give and the length of notice the employee is entitled to if their contract of employment is terminated.

- The job title which applies to the employee and the work that they are engaged to do.

- The place of work or an indication that the employee may be required to work at various locations.

- The details of any collective agreements which directly affect the terms and conditions of the employee.

- *The details of any disciplinary rules which apply to the employee.*

- *The need to specify a person with whom the employee can raise a grievance connected with their employment or any disciplinary decision affecting them.*

- *The need to identify a person to whom an employee can go to when seeking redress on any grievance relating to their employment.*

- *The need to include a statement indicating whether a pensions contracting out certificate is in force for the employment.*

The clauses listed above are the minimum required by the Employment Protection (Consolidation) Act 1978. In practice, the Contract of Employment can be as long and as complex as the employer and employee choose.

Statement of Terms and Conditions of Employment

In the absence of a Contract of Employment, check whether the employee has been given a Statement of Terms and Conditions of Employment. Every employer is required by law to issue this statement to employees within two months of the date of commencement of employment; it covers broadly the same headings. In the absence of a Contract of Employment, the Statement of Terms and Conditions of Employment should give you the guidance you need.
A Statement of Terms and Conditions is legally required unless:

- The employee will be working for less than a month, or
- The employee normally works less than 8 hours a week.

The Statement must set out each of the required terms in full. Employers are not allowed to refer employees to other documents that deal with Terms of Employment unless they are terms and conditions relating to sickness, injury or pension schemes. In these matters, employees may be referred to a document which he/she has a reasonable opportunity of reading.

It is important that the payroll office is notified of any variations in Contracts of Employment because benefits bestowed by the revised contract could be taxable and reportable to the Inland Revenue. Failure to deduct tax or report these benefits could attract a fine for the business.

Written Pay Statements

The Employment Protection (Consolidation) Act stipulates that every employee has the right to be told how his/her pay is calculated. The employee is entitled to be told:

- the gross wage or salary
- the amount and purpose of each deduction
- the net wage or salary.

Here is an example.

Pay Advice for week ending 28/2/1997

Employee's Name	B Gates
Date	28/2/97
Week	48
Tax Code	376L
Employee No	14

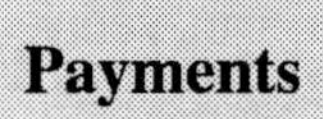

Payments

	£	£
Basic	465.00	
Overtime	-	
Bonus	-	
Sick Pay	-	
Maternity Pay	-	
	Total Payments	465.00

Deductions

	£	
PAYE	91.52	
NI	40.62	
Pension	-	
	Total Deductions	132.14
	Net Pay for Week	**332.86**

Supplementary Information

Total Gross Pay this week	465.00
Earnings for NI this week	465.00
Earnings for NI YTD	21877.50
NI Paid to date	1914.11
Gross Earnings for Tax this week	465.00
Gross Pay for Tax YTD	25378.00
Tax Paid to date	5111.52
Pension Payments to date	Nil

Employee Records

Government legislation requires employers to maintain records. Much of this record keeping is the responsibility of the payroll department. Increasingly, failure to keep (or submit) records now attracts automatic fines which can be very expensive.

Many of these records are kept on official forms and returns. Details of these forms and how to complete them are given in the appropriate section of the book. The purpose of this section is to provide a broad overview of the kinds of employee records which affect the payroll function.

Pay As You Earn

The legal requirements for Pay As You Earn (PAYE) record keeping is given on Card 9 of the Employer's Quick Guide to Pay As You Earn and National Insurance Contributions CWG1 (April 1997).

You need to keep a record of gross pay and PAYE deductions. These details must be entered on the employee's P11 which must be kept for at least three years after the tax year to which the records relate.

You must complete the end of year returns which are made on forms P14 and form P35 (see Section 8). Many PAYE records are summaries of the deductions made on form P11. It is important, therefore, that P11 forms are completed conscientiously.

You will also need to keep records of expenses and benefits in kind paid to directors and others earning over £8,500. Expenses and benefits should be recorded on form P11D at the end of every tax year which should be sent to the Inland Revenue by 6 July together with form P11D(b).

You also have to complete and submit a form P9D listing expenses and benefits for employees earning less than £8,500 per annum. This means that you need an expenses and benefits recording system capable of gathering the information you need. See Section 9 for more details on expenses and benefits information required.

National Insurance Records

Employees' national insurance records divide into two main areas. These are Class 1 deductions and Class 1A deductions.

Class 1 National Insurance is a deduction from pay which has to be recorded on the employee's form P11. National Insurance is subject to the same monthly and yearly reporting procedures as PAYE. Details of Class 1 National Insurance Contributions (NICs) are given in Section 12.

Class 1A NICs are paid by the employer on car benefits enjoyed by employees during the previous tax year. Details are contained in Section 9. Both employer and employees will need to keep records of the make and model of the company car, type of fuel, business mileage etc.

Statutory Sick Pay

The employer is also required to keep records relating to Statutory Sick Pay. Details are given in Section 13. Employers are required by law to keep records of:

- All periods of sickness lasting four calendar days or more which are reported by employees.

- Statutory Sickness Payments made to employees.

- Statutory Sickness Pay recovered under the percentage threshold scheme.

The employer has to keep these records even if he pays the employee normal wages during the period of sickness. Failure to pay valid statutory sick pay is punishable by a fine. Employer's legal responsibilities are listed in the DSS Statutory Sick Pay manual.

Statutory Maternity Pay

Rights of pregnant women were considerably extended and enhanced in 1994. Pregnant women are entitled to maternity pay, maternity leave, protection against unfair dismissal and time off for antenatal care. This workbook is only concerned with Statutory Maternity Pay. If you need to know about the other legal aspects, we suggest you consult an excellent Department of Trade and Industry/Social Security booklet called 'Maternity Rights PL958 - A Guide for Employers and Employees', obtainable free from Cambertown Ltd, Unit 8 Commercial Road, Gowthorpe Industrial Estate, Gowthorpe, Rotherham, SG3 9BL - telephone 01709-888688.

You are required by law to keep medical proof of pregnancy for any employees who have received Statutory Maternity Pay (SMP). You also need to keep records of the dates of maternity absence notified by employees and record any weeks when SMP was *not* paid with reasons why the SMP was not paid.

The rules covering Statutory Maternity Pay are contained in the Contributions Agency booklet CA29 from April 1997 called Statutory Maternity Pay Manual for Employers. In general terms, failure to pay Statutory Maternity Pay, failure to keep records, or failure to co-operate with an Appeals Tribunal is punishable by a fine of up to £1,000. Falsely claiming Statutory Maternity Pay can lead to fines of up to £5,000.

Non Statutory Payroll Deductions

Employers are required by law to deduct tax and national insurance from employees' wages. However, many employees volunteer to have *additional* deductions taken from their salaries. These deductions include pension contributions, Save As You Earn, Payroll Giving etc. Many voluntary deductions have tax implications. This means that you have to keep deductions records which can be scrutinised by the Inland Revenue or DSS inspectors.

All payroll deductions must be fully recorded to prove that there has been neither tax evasion nor fraud. Check the design of your payment advice slips to ensure that every slip contains a complete list of all types of deductions. You will also need to say whether the deduction was taken before, or after, tax. A record of duplicate payslips should help defend you against accusations of poor record keeping.

The Data Protection Act 1984

About the Act

The Data Protection Act is intended to protect an individual's privacy. It enables them to find out what information is being held about themselves, challenge it if necessary and claim compensation in certain circumstances.

Organisations storing sensitive information about individuals on computers are required to register. Failure to register is a criminal offence punishable by an unlimited fine. It is also a criminal offence to hold data in a way which has not been disclosed to the Data Registrar.

You can register your business by requesting a registration pack from the Data Protection Registrar, Wycliffe House, Water Lane, Wilmslow, Cheshire, SK9 5AF, Tel: 01625-545745, Fax: 01625-524510.

Registration lasts three years. At the time of writing these notes, the registration fee was £75. The Data Protection Registry produces an excellent guide to the Data Protection Act which is simply called 'The Guidelines'. You will need to consult this booklet to explore the fine print.

Do I Need to Register?

The Data Protection Act only applies to information stored on a computer so if you do payroll calculations by hand, the Act doesn't apply to you.

If you do your payroll calculations on a computer, you are also exempt *provided your payroll data is limited to:*

- Calculating amounts payable as remuneration for service in any employment or office
- Calculating amounts payable as pensions for service in any employment or office
- Paying remuneration or pensions
- Paying amounts deducted from remuneration or pensions.

You are only allowed to release this information to certain outside bodies, eg tax authorities, courts, national security etc.

Although you are exempt in theory, in practice it is extremely easy to breach the conditions of the exemption. For example:

- Using time keeping records to judge an employee's performance is a breach of the exemption
- Using payroll deductions as an indicator of trade union membership would be illegal
- Using 'date of birth' to decide on an early retirement programme would also breach the Act.

You are likely to fall foul of the Act if your payroll program is linked to personnel files also stored on computer. This would make it impossible to rely on the exemption from the Act. Too much information would be available to too many people who could use the information in a wide variety of ways.

In practice, most computer users will choose to register. Even if today's circumstances qualify for an exemption, who knows what changes will infiltrate the payroll system in future years? Any of these changes could invalidate the exemption. It is easier to register rather than have to constantly monitor compliance.

Other Legal Aspects

According to the size of the business, you may also need:

- A system of keeping personnel records
- An Equal Opportunities policy
- A Health and Safety policy
- Employer Liability Insurance.

In most large organisations, these will be the responsibility of the Personnel (or Human Resources) department. However, in small businesses, these could be assigned to the admin/payroll staff.

Payroll Documentation

There is a legal requirement for payroll documentation to be retained by the employer for at least three years after the tax year to which they relate. Some system for filing and retaining these records should, therefore, be put in place.

Payment of Wages

Employees can be paid by any method acceptable to both the employer and the employee. Wages can be paid by cash, cheque, credit transfer or BACS. Following the repeal of the Truck Acts, employers cannot be forced to pay wages in cash should they decide not to do so.

Industrial Relations Law

Minimum rates of pay are sometimes negotiated between employers and trade unions. These rates of pay may form part of the employee's Contract of Employment. As such, the employer may be bound contractually to keep the employee's wages in line with national agreements.

Discrimination and Equal Pay

According to the Equal Pay Act 1970, it is illegal to discriminate against anyone on the grounds of race, sex or trade union activities. For example, it is illegal to pay men and women different rates of pay for the same work.

Equal work means equal pay!

Simple Manual PAYE Calculations

Every employer is required by law to deduct both income tax and national insurance contributions from employees' earnings. In this section, we concentrate on income tax deductions. We will look at national insurance deductions in Section 12.

Payroll deductions are normally taken weekly or monthly according to how frequently wages are paid. Monthly wages are attractive to the employer since they only involve 12 wage calculations per annum instead of the 52 calculations required if employees are paid weekly.

To understand how PAYE works, we first need to understand personal allowances; these are explained below.

Personal Allowances

Everyone in Britain is allowed to earn a certain amount of money free of income tax. This is called the personal allowance. The following table lists the personal allowances for the 1997/98 tax year.

	£
Personal	4045
Personal (65-74)	5220
Personal (75 and over)	5400
Married Couple's	1830*
Married Couple's (65-74)	3185*
Married Couple's (75 and over)	3225*
Additional Personal	1830*
Widow's Bereavement	1830*
Blind Person	1280

* (Restricted to 15% relief - explained on pages 30 and 31)

Notice that there are three levels of personal allowances depending upon the age of the taxpayer (ie under 65, between 65 and 75, and over 75 years of age). In this book, we will focus on persons of normal working age so all of our examples will use the personal allowance relating to people under 65 years of age (£4045 for 1997/98).

Married couples are allowed to claim an additional allowance. This allowance can be claimed by the husband, or by the wife, or the allowance can be shared between them. Once again, the level of the marriage allowance depends on the age of the partners. We will use the marriage allowance for partners under 65 years of age in our computations. This was set at £1830 for the 1997/98 tax year.

Persons who are registered as blind with their local authority are entitled to claim an additional allowance of £1280 for the 1997/98 tax year.

The employee's tax code is calculated by the Inland Revenue based on information submitted on the employee's tax return (form SA100 Schedule E1). The Inland Revenue then notify the employer of the employee's tax code on P6(T) (see page 38). The tax code is the amount of tax free pay that the employee is allowed to earn with the final digit removed. For example, the single person's personal allowance is £4045. This means that they would be allowed to earn £4045 free of income tax. Assuming that there are no other allowances or benefits, that person's tax code would be 404L. The L stands for 'lower', ie single person's allowance.

Restricted Allowances

Notice that certain allowances have an asterisk* alongside them. This means that they are restricted to 15% tax relief. The value of a restricted allowance is the same, irrespective of a tax payer's personal circumstances. Here is an example based on the married couple's allowance of £1830 for the 1997/98 tax year.

If the allowance is restricted to 15% then the allowance is worth:

£1830 allowance @ 15% = £274.50 of tax saved.

If the allowance wasn't restricted to 15% and the employee is a standard rate tax payer then the allowance would be worth:

£1830 allowance @ 23% = £420.90 of tax saved.

If the employee is a higher rate tax payer then the allowance would be worth:

£1830 allowance @ 40% = £732.00 of tax saved.

Restricting the value of an allowance to 15% means that the allowance is worth the same to all taxpayers, irrespective of their personal circumstances.

Tax Rates

Once an employee has taken his share of tax free income then income tax is applied to the balance at a progressively steeper rate. These rates are shown in the following table.

Taxable Income £	**Rate**	**%**	**Band Width**
Up to 4100	Lower Rate	20	4,100
4101 - 26100	Basic Rate	23	22,000
over 26100	Higher Rate	40	-

For example, a single person earning £35,000 per annum with a tax code of 404L would pay:

	Earnings £	**Tax Rate** %	**Tax Paid** £
First	4045	Tax free	Nil
Next	4100	20	820
Next	22000	23	5060
Next	4855	40	1942
Total Earnings	35000	**Total Tax Paid**	7822

The calculation shows the total amount of tax paid in a year. Employed people, however, usually pay on a weekly or monthly basis. This means that some method of calculating weekly or monthly tax deductions is needed. This method is, of course, Pay As You Earn (PAYE). Here are some notes on administering PAYE.

Calculating PAYE Income Tax

Before the second world war, income tax was collected on an annual basis very much along the lines of the calculation shown above. However, there were two disadvantages.

- The government had to wait until the end of the year to collect the tax due to them

- Tax payers often spent their income. They then had difficulty paying the tax bill when it finally arrived.

To overcome these difficulties, the government devised the system of Pay As You Earn. PAYE only applies to employed people (self employed people are still assessed and taxed on an annual basis). In broad principle, PAYE income tax is collected each time the employee is paid. This means that the annual income is sliced into weekly or monthly amounts. Each weekly or monthly slice of income is then allocated a proportion of the annual tax free pay and tax is levied on the balance. To simplify the calculations, the government gives employers tax tables and forms at the beginning of each tax year. We will see how to use these tables shortly.

The tax tables, forms and instructions are contained in the 'Employer's Annual Pack'. A copy of this pack has been reproduced on the accompanying CD. Here is a brief introduction to the main forms and manuals.

Working out PAYE!

Employer's Quick Guide to PAYE and National Insurance Contributions

These instructions are contained in a set of 22 numbered cards. Be sure that you have an up-to-date set to hand. Where we refer to a topic which is also covered on 'the cards', we will show the card number so that you can easily check it out. The cards carry the reference number CWG1 April 1997.

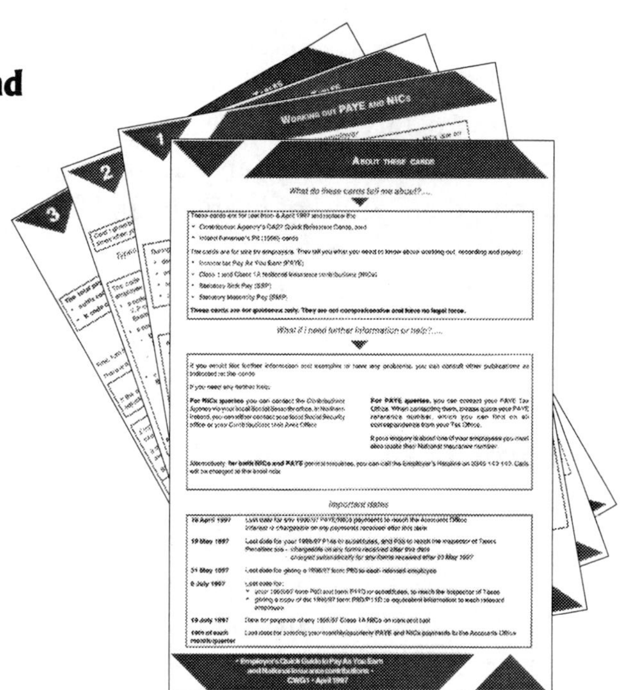

Employer's Further Guide to PAYE and NICs

This booklet contains more detailed information than the Quick Guide. If you have a problem, it is well worthwhile checking the guide. Until April 1997, both the Inland Revenue and the Contributions Agency had their own guides. These were the 'Employer's Further Guide to PAYE P7' and the 'Employer's Manual on National Insurance Contributions CA28'. These have been replaced by the combined 'Employer's Further Guide to PAYE and NICs CWG2'(1997). Where we deal with a topic in this workbook which is covered in the guide, we will point out the relevant section.

In addition to the two guides mentioned above, you will also need:

- One form P11 (1997) per employee
- A set of Pay Adjustment Tables (Tables A - 1993 Issue)
- A set of Taxable Pay Tables (Tables LR + B to D - 1997 Issue)
- Expenses and Benefits Tax Guide (480 - 1997)
- Copies of forms P14, P35, P11D, P9D, P45, P46 and P11D(b).

Check that you have all the forms and guides listed above. If you are missing anything before 26 July 1997, call the Annual Pack Orderline on 0345-646-646. After that date, order your materials through your PAYE tax office or Contributions Agency, as appropriate. A list of useful Inland Revenue forms and guides is given in Appendix 1.

P11s and Tables A and Tables LR + B to D are explained in a little more detail below.

Form P11

You need one of these forms for each employee. Have a look at the example on page 41. Notice that there is space on the top right of the form for the employee's details. The full name, date of birth and national insurance number are very important because these details are used by both you and the tax office to uniquely identify each employee. This is important because the employee's record of social security contributions is based on your P11 records. Failure to properly record payments could jeopardise your employees' future entitlements to benefits.

Columns located to the right of the central date column on the P11 are to record Income Tax deductions. Columns to the left of the central date column on the P11 are to record National Insurance deductions.

Notice that the centre of the form contains a list of tax months and tax weeks. Unfortunately, the P11 only shows week and month *numbers*. There is no indication of the *dates* to which these numbers relate. To understand the significance of the week or month number, you have to look at an Income Tax Calendar. You can use the dates shown on the back of card 5 of the Employer's Quick Guide to Pay As You Earn and National Insurance contributions or use the table on page 35. If a payment falls between the dates shown in the 'Period Covered (both dates inclusive)' column then use that week or month number for your tax calculation. For example, if you pay your staff weekly and a payment falls on 22 July then you would use the table relating to Week 16.

Income Tax Calendar

Weeks

Week No	Period Covered (both dates inclusive)	Week No	Period Covered (both dates inclusive)
1	April 6 - 12	30	Oct 26 - Nov 1
2	April 13 - 19	31	Nov 2 - 8
3	April 20 - 26	32	Nov 9 - 15
4	April 27 - May 3	33	Nov 16 - 22
5	May 4 - 10	34	Nov 23 - 29
6	May 11 - 17	35	Nov 30 - Dec 6
7	May 18 - 24	36	Dec 7 - 13
8	May 25 - 31	37	Dec 14 - 20
9	June 1 - 7	38	Dec 21 - 27
10	June 8 - 14	39	Dec 28 - Jan 3
11	June 15 - 21	40	Jan 4 - 10
12	June 22 - 28	41	Jan 11 - 17
13	June 29 - July 5	42	Jan 18 - 24
14	July 6 - 12	43	Jan 25 - 31
15	July 13 - 19	44	Feb 1 - 7
16	July 20 - 26	45	Feb 8 - 14
17	July 27 - Aug 2	46	Feb 15 - 21
18	Aug 3 - 9	47	Feb 22 - 28
19	Aug 10 - 16		
20	Aug 17 - 23		
21	Aug 24 - 30		
22	Aug 31 - Sep 6		
23	Sep 7 - 13		
24	Sep 14 - 20		
25	Sep 21 - 27		
26	Sep 28 - Oct 4		
27	Oct 5 - 11		
28	Oct 12 - 18		
29	Oct 19 - 25		

Week No	Normal Years	Leap Years
48	Mar 1 - 7	Feb 29 - Mar 6
49	Mar 8 - 14	Mar 7 - 13
50	Mar 15 - 21	Mar 14 - 20
51	Mar 22 - 28	Mar 21 - 27
52	Mar 29-Apr 4	Mar 28 - Apr 3
53	April 5	April 4 - 5

Months

Month No	Period Covered (both dates inclusive)	Month No	Period Covered (both dates inclusive)
1	April 6 - May 5	7	Oct 6 - Nov 5
2	May 6 - June 5	8	Nov 6 - Dec 5
3	June 6 - July 5	9	Dec 6 - Jan 5
4	July 6 - Aug 5	10	Jan 6 - Feb 5
5	Aug 6 - Sept 5	11	Feb 6 - Mar 5
6	Sept 6 - Oct 5	12	Mar 6 - Apr 5

Pay Adjustment Tables (Tables A)

These tables allow the employer to calculate the amount of tax free pay available to an employee in any week or month. The tax free pay is not all given to the employee in one lump sum at the beginning of the tax year. It is shared out over the weeks or months when the employee gets paid. An example of the contents of Tables A is shown on pages 182-183. The tables are divided into two sections. The first set of tables is for weekly paid employees. The second set of tables (towards the back of the booklet) is for monthly paid employees. The tables are very easy to use. Simply choose a week or month, look up the employee's tax code and read off the total tax free pay to date. We will look at an example of how to do this shortly.

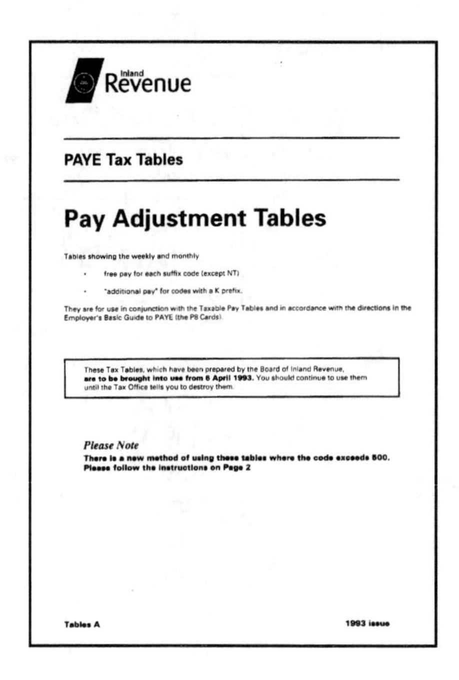

Inland Revenue

PAYE Tax Tables

Pay Adjustment Tables

Tables showing the weekly and monthly

- free pay for each suffix code (except NT)
- "additional pay" for codes with a K prefix.

They are for use in conjunction with the Taxable Pay Tables and in accordance with the directions in the Employer's Basic Guide to PAYE (the P8 Cards).

These Tax Tables, which have been prepared by the Board of Inland Revenue, **are to be brought into use from 6 April 1993.** You should continue to use them until the Tax Office tells you to destroy them.

Please Note
There is a new method of using these tables where the code exceeds 500. Please follow the instructions on Page 2

Tables A **1993 issue**

Taxable Pay Tables (Tables LR + B to D)

These are used to calculate the amount of tax due. There are four types of tables:

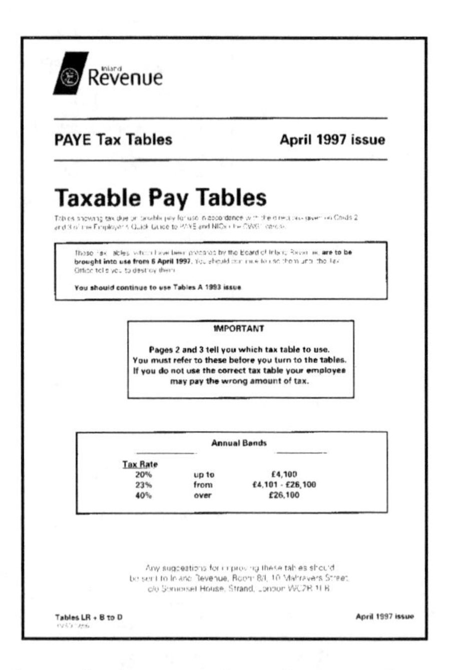

Inland Revenue

PAYE Tax Tables April 1997 issue

Taxable Pay Tables

Tables showing tax due on taxable pay for use in accordance with the directions given on Cards 2 and 3 of the Employer's Quick Guide to PAYE and NICs [illegible]

These Tax Tables, which have been prepared by the Board of Inland Revenue, **are to be brought into use from 6 April 1997.** You should continue to use them until the Tax Office tells you to destroy them.

You should continue to use Tables A 1993 issue

IMPORTANT

Pages 2 and 3 tell you which tax table to use. You must refer to these before you turn to the tables. If you do not use the correct tax table your employee may pay the wrong amount of tax.

Annual Bands

Tax Rate		
20%	up to	£4,100
23%	from	£4,101 - £26,100
40%	over	£26,100

Any suggestions for improving these tables should be sent to Inland Revenue, Room 8/1, 10 Maltravers Street, c/o Somerset House, Strand, London WC2R 1LB

Tables LR + B to D **April 1997 issue**

Table LR - This is used where the employee's taxable pay falls wholly within the lower rate tax banding. This means that all pay is taxed at 20%.

Table B - This table applies where the employee's taxable pay is high enough to attract basic rate tax which is currently 23%.

Table C - This applies where the employee's taxable income is high enough to take them into the higher tax rate band of 40%.

Table D - This table applies if the *whole* of the employee's income is to be taxed at 40%. This would usually apply where the employee has an income from another source which has already used up his or her allowances and has, therefore, accounted for all tax at the lower and basic rate tax bands.

Simple Payroll Example

Bill Gates

Let's have a look now at how we would calculate income tax for an imaginary employee called Bill Gates.

We will assume that he is on our payroll at the start of the new tax year. We should have received from the Inland Revenue a notice of coding on form P6(T) (see example on page 38).

You will remember that Bill Gates' tax code has been generated as a result of the employee completing his annual tax return. The Inland Revenue then allocates a tax code based on the information supplied by Bill. Agreeing the tax code is entirely the responsibility of the Inland Revenue and the employee. The employer is not part of that process. The employer is not authorised to alter the tax code in any way. If the employee has a problem with his code, it is up to him to get the problem resolved by talking directly to the Inland Revenue.

We will use the Deductions Working sheet shown on page 41. We will use the Table A and Tables LR + B to D shown in Appendix 2. We will also assume that we are starting our calculations for a new tax year and that Bill Gates was already on the payroll at the start of the tax year. We have entered Bill's details on the top of the form. His tax code is 524H (ie slightly more than a single person's allowance).

Step1 At the end of the first month, his pay is £1100. This is entered in column 2 on the fourth line (opposite month 1).

Step 2 Enter the total pay to date in column 3, ie £1100. (This is the cumulative total pay for the tax year).

Contd

Form P6(T)

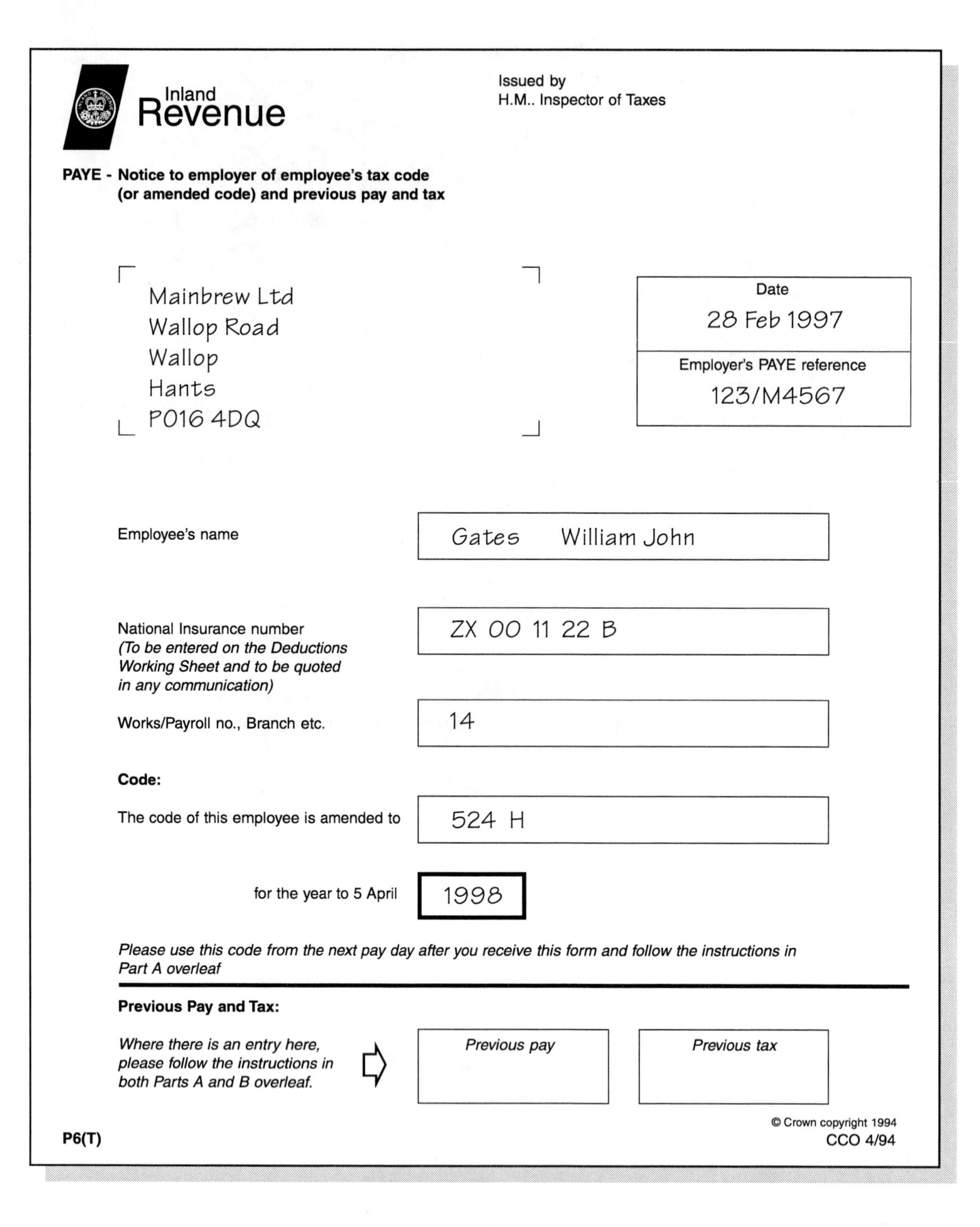

Inland Revenue

Issued by
H.M.. Inspector of Taxes

PAYE - Notice to employer of employee's tax code (or amended code) and previous pay and tax

Mainbrew Ltd
Wallop Road
Wallop
Hants
PO16 4DQ

Date
28 Feb 1997
Employer's PAYE reference
123/M4567

Employee's name	Gates William John
National Insurance number *(To be entered on the Deductions Working Sheet and to be quoted in any communication)*	ZX 00 11 22 B
Works/Payroll no., Branch etc.	14

Code:

The code of this employee is amended to	524 H
for the year to 5 April	1998

Please use this code from the next pay day after you receive this form and follow the instructions in Part A overleaf

Previous Pay and Tax:

Where there is an entry here, please follow the instructions in both Parts A and B overleaf.

Previous pay	*Previous tax*

P6(T)

CCO 4/94

Example (Contd)

Step 3 To calculate column 4a, look at the 'Pay Adjustment Tables - Tables A' (see examples in Appendix 2 on pages 182 and 183) and find Month 1 Table A - Pay Adjustment. You will see that the tax codes on the left hand side of each column run from 0 to 500. Alongside each tax code is a 'Total pay adjustment to date' figure. For example, someone with a tax code of 100 would be allowed to earn £84.09 free of tax in the first month of the tax year. Let's see how to deal with Bill Gates' tax code of 524.

Since the tax code exceeds 500, we need to use the box contained in the bottom right hand corner of the tax tables. The instructions in the box tell us to subtract 500 from the tax code and look up the excess in the tables. In this example, Bill Gates' code is 524 so we need to look up 24 (ie 524 - 500) in the body of the monthly tax tables as follows:

	£
Tax free pay on 24	20.75
Tax free pay on 500	416.67
Total free pay for Month 1	437.42

Enter £437.42 in column 4a.

Step 4 Deduct column 4a from column 3 and enter the total taxable pay to date in column 5, ie £1100 - £437.42 = £662.58. Ignore column 4b totally for the present.

Step 5 We now need to calculate the tax due at the end of month 1. Because there are several rates of income tax, ie 20%, 23% and 40%, there are several tax tables. These are labelled 'Taxable Pay Tables - Tables LR + B to D'.

To check which tax table to use, we need to look at the first two pages of the Taxable Pay Tables LR + B to D. One table is for weekly paid people, the other is for monthly paid persons. Since Bill Gates is paid monthly, we need to use the 'Pay at Monthly Rates' table reproduced in this workbook on page 184. Bill Gates' taxable pay in month 1 exceeds £342 (first column) but does not exceed £2175 (centre column) which means we now need to turn to Table B.

Contd

Example (Contd)

Step 6 Table B shows tax rates of 23% - see example on page 186. Note that there is no entry for £662.58. This means that we will have to break the amount into two elements of £600 and £62. At this stage in the calculation, we ignore pence (we do not round up or round down). These amounts yield tax payable as follows:

	£
Tax on £600 =	138.00
Tax on £62 =	14.26
Total tax due =	152.26

Step 7 £152.26 represents the tax on £662, assuming that the whole of the tax was charged at 23%. However, remember that everyone is entitled to pay tax at 20% on the first £4100 of taxable income. Clearly, the taxpayer has been overcharged and is entitled to some form of rebate. This rebate can be read off from Table B - Lower Rate Relief (see page 187). You will see that, for month 1, you need to *subtract* £10.25 from the value calculated so far. The tax due from Bill Gates will, therefore, amount to:

£152.26 - £10.25 = £142.01

Enter this amount in column 6. Since this is the first month of the tax year, you can enter the same amount in column 7. Ignore columns 6a and 6b for now.

This completes the first month's entries. Continue working out the deductions for the second month as follows.

Step 8 Enter the pay for the month, say £1200, in column 2 for month 2.

Step 9 Total pay to date in column 3 comprises this month's pay plus the previous month's pay, ie £1200 + £1100 = £2300.

Step 10 Look up 'Table A - pay adjustment' for month 2, tax code 524 (see page 183). Enter the amount in column 4a, ie £874.84.

Contd

Deductions Working Sheet P11 Year to 5 April 19__

...o forenames William John

...rks no. etc 14

Date of starting *in figures* Day | Month | Year

Date of leaving *in figures* Day | Month | Year

National Insurance contributions

For guidance on National Insurance and the completion of columns 1a to 1h see CA27 Quick Reference Cards

For guidance on Statutory Sick Pay figures see leaflet CA30

For guidance on Statutory Maternity Pay figures see leaflet CA29

***or** contact Social Security Advice Line for Employers - telephone number is in CA 2*

At the top of each section in the NI Tables there is a letter, for examp *or E.* Copy that letter from the Table you use to the box bottom left o overleaf. If the employee's circumstances change part way through a change as well. Record all letters with separate totals for each table *Insurance Contributions'* Remember to record under letter Y any Class 1a on the last line of th See the *CA27 Quick Reference Cards* for further information exa

Earnings recorded in column 1a should not exceed the Upper Earnings Limit

For employer's use	Earnings on which employee's contributions payable *Whole pounds only* 1a £	Total of employee's and employer's contributions payable 1b £	Employee's contribution payable 1c £	Earnings on which employee's contributions at contracted-out rate payable included in col. 1a *Whole pounds only* 1d £	Em con con rate colu 1e	K codes only: Tax due at end of current period Mark refunds 'R' 6a £	K codes only: Regulatory limit i.e. 50% of column 2 entry 6b £	Tax deducted or refunded in the week or month. Mark refunds 'R' 7 £	K codes only: Tax not deducted owing to the Regulatory limit 8 £	For employer's use
								Steps 6-7 Page 40		
								142 01		
								165 24		
								Step 13 Page 43		
	Total c/fwd	Total c/fwd	Total c/fwd	Total c/fwd	T					

P11(1997)

† If amended cross out previous code.

Ø If any week/month the amount in column 4a is more than the amount in column 3, leave column 5 blank.

Employee's surname *in CAPITALS*	First two forenames
National Insurance no.	Date of birth *in figures* Day Month Year
Works no. etc	Date of starting *in figures* Day Month Year

Tax code †	Amended code †				
	Wk/Mth in which applied				

Date of leaving *in figures*
Day Month Year

ne Tax

		K codes only			K codes only			K codes only	
Total pay to date	Total free pay to date (Table A)	Total 'additional pay' to date (Table A)	Total taxable pay to date i.e. column 3 *minus* column 4a **or** column 3 *plus* column 4b	Total tax due to date as shown by Taxable Pay Tables	Tax due at end of current period Mark refunds 'R'	Regulatory limit i.e. 50% of column 2 entry	Tax deducted or refunded in the week or month. Mark refunds 'R'	Tax not deducted owing to the Regulatory limit	For employer's use
3	4a	4b	5	6	6a	6b	7	8	
£	£	£	£	£	£	£	£	£	

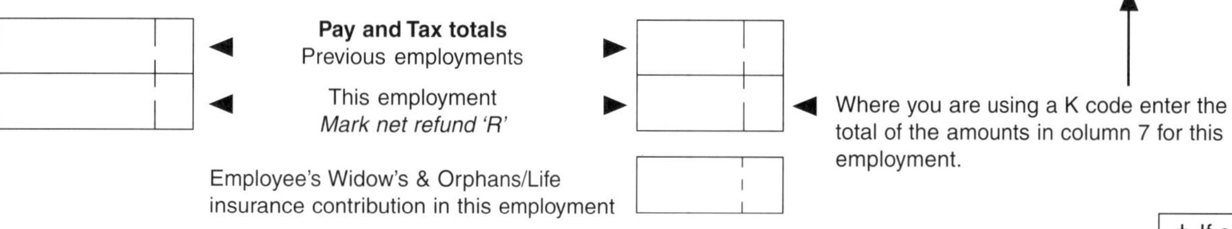

Pay and Tax totals
Previous employments

This employment
Mark net refund 'R'

Employee's Widow's & Orphans/Life insurance contribution in this employment

Where you are using a K code enter the total of the amounts in column 7 for this employment.

† If amended cross out previous code.

§ Complete this line if pay day falls on 5 April (in leap years 4 & 5 April).

ars after the end of the year to which it relates, or longer if you are asked to so so.

Example (Contd)

Step 11 Deduct column 4a from column 3 and enter the amount in column 5, ie £2300.00 - £874.84 = £1425.16. Check whether this amount falls within Table B (see page 184) - which it does.

Step 12 Look up 'Taxable Pay Tables - Table B' and note the total tax due to date for taxable pay of £1425.16. The value is made up of the following amounts:

£322 + £5.75 - £20.50 = £307.25

Remember to deduct the lower rate relief!
Enter this amount in column 6.

Step 13 Remember PAYE is normally calculated on a cumulative basis (ie we are working out 'total tax due to date on total pay'). If we subtracted £307.25 from Bill Gates' pay in Month 2, he would not be very happy as this is ***total*** tax due on £2300 pay. We must give credit for the tax already paid in Month 1, ie £142.01. The correct amount of tax to deduct is, therefore:

£307.25 less £142.01 = £165.24

Enter this amount in column 7.

Exercise 1

Calculate Bill Gates pay for June, July and August as follows:

Pay on	30 June	£1400
	31 July	£1250
	31 Aug	£1500

Hint: In case you don't have access to a full set of pay adjustment tables, the following may be useful.

Month	Table A Code 524H Pay Adjustment
	£
1	437.42
2	874.84
3	1312.26
4	1749.68
5	2187.10

Tables LR and B to D are to be found between pages 184 and 189 of this book. Use these to work out the tax due.

Check your answer with page 198.

How to Pay Over the Tax Collected to the Inland Revenue

Amounts deducted from an employee's wages have to be paid over to the Inland Revenue according to the times shown below. For example, if you paid your staff on the 30th of April, this would occur in tax month 1 (which runs from 6 April to 5 May). Tax (and national insurance) collected from the employee's salary in tax month 1 has to be paid over to the Inland Revenue by 19 May.

Paying Taxes

Tax Month	Deductions in these Periods:	Are paid to Inland Revenue by:
1	6 April - 5 May	19 May
2	6 May - 5 June	19 June
3	6 June - 5 July	19 July
4	6 July - 5 Aug	19 Aug
5	6 Aug - 5 Sep	19 Sep
6	6 Sep - 5 Oct	19 Oct
7	6 Oct - 5 Nov	19 Nov
8	6 Nov - 5 Dec	19 Dec
9	6 Dec - 5 Jan	19 Jan
10	6 Jan - 5 Feb	19 Feb
11	6 Feb - 5 Mar	19 Mar
12	6 Mar - 5 April	19 April

The Inland Revenue serves as a tax collector for both PAYE collections and National Insurance Contributions. Send the tax collected to the Inland Revenue with one payslip from booklet P30BC. An example of the cover, payslip and record of payments form from booklet P30BC is shown on page 46. Note that the payslip has spaces to record the amount of income tax and the amount of net national insurance collected. National insurance contributions are labelled 'Net National Insurance' because the amount remitted is the difference between the national insurance collected, and the national insurance paid out as Statutory Sick Pay or Statutory Maternity Pay. Don't worry about National Insurance yet, it is covered in Section 12.

In addition to the payslip booklet, the Inland Revenue provides you with another form which enables you to keep track of how much you have paid. The form summarises the amounts paid in. This is form P32(1997) (see example of this form on page 47). If the level of payments is small (ie below £600 per month for both PAYE and NIC combined), the employer can pay the Inland Revenue quarterly.

Front Cover of Payslip Book P30BC

Inland Revenue

PAYSLIP BOOKLET

- Income Tax - Pay As You Earn
- National Insurance Contributions
- Amounts deductible from payments to Sub-Contractors in the Construction Industry

Collection reference

Income Tax Year **Months**

Your reference

Date Booklet Printed:

The enclosed payslips are for your use in making payments of Income Tax (including any amounts deductible from sub-contractors) and National Insurance Contributions for the above year. Each payslip shows the period covered and the date on which payment is due.

Interest will be charged on amounts not paid by 19 April following the end of the tax year to which they relate.

Before making payment please read the notes on pages 2 and 3.

Collector of Taxes

Accounts Office Shipley
BRADFORD
West Yorkshire BD98 8AA
Telephone:
Bradford 530750 (STD 01274)

P30BC

If any of the above details are incorrect or change, please complete and return the form on the back cover.

Page 1

Example of Payslip in Book P30BC

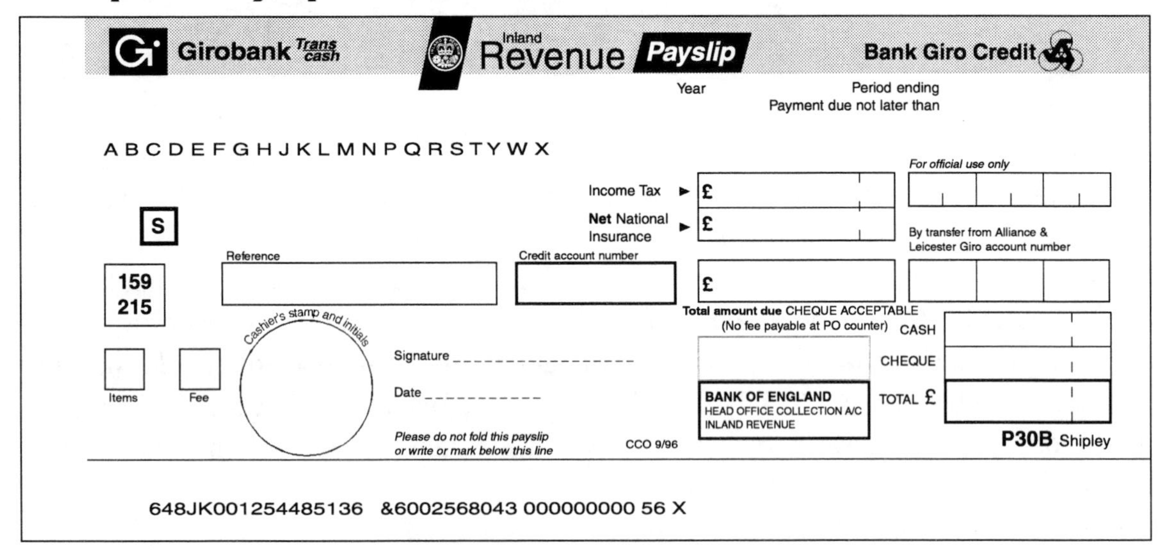

Girobank Trans cash

Inland Revenue **Payslip**

Bank Giro Credit

Year

Period ending
Payment due not later than

A B C D E F G H J K L M N P Q R S T Y W X

For official use only

S

Income Tax ► £

Net National Insurance ► £

By transfer from Alliance & Leicester Giro account number

159
215

Reference

Credit account number

£

Total amount due CHEQUE ACCEPTABLE
(No fee payable at PO counter)

Cashier's stamp and initials

CASH

Signature

CHEQUE

Items

Fee

Date

BANK OF ENGLAND
HEAD OFFICE COLLECTION A/C
INLAND REVENUE

TOTAL £

Please do not fold this payslip or write or mark below this line

CCO 9/96

P30B Shipley

648JK001254485136 &6002568043 000000000 56 X

Example of 'Record of Payments' Form from Payslip Book P30BC

Record of Payments

You are advised to complete the record below each time you make a payment. This information will be required when you complete the Employer's Annual Return.

Period ending	**1** Income Tax £	**2** Gross National Insurance £	**3** Total Deductions *Amount from col.5,page 4* £	**4** Net National Insurance *(2 less 3)* £	**5** Total Amount Due *(1 + 4)* £	Date Paid
5 May						
5 Jun						
5 Jul						
5 Aug						
5 Sep						
5 Oct						
5 Nov						
5 Dec						
5 Jan						
5 Feb						
5 Mar						
5 Apr						
Total						

Form P32(1997)

Inland Revenue

Employer's Payment Record

Employer's name

Collection Office reference
P

Please enter the tax year for which you are making the payments here
19 -

You will need information about payments when you complete your form P35 (Employer's Annual Return).
Please enter the details requested each time you make a payment. For example, suppose you make quarterly payments. You would record the details every third month when you make the payment. Or if you prefer you can enter details for each month (or week) and total them every third month.

Payments for last year's Class 1A National Insurance, unless paid by the Alternative Payment Method, should be included in column 8.

Period	Week no.	Total Statutory Sick Pay (SSP) paid 1	Total SSP recovered 2	Statutory Maternity Pay (SMP) paid 3	Total SMP recovered 4	NIC compensation on SMP (if due) 5	NIC Holiday claimed 6	Total deductions *add 2, 4, 5 and 6* 7	Gross National Insurance 8	Net National Insurance *8 less 7* 9	PAYE income tax 10	Total amount due *add 9 and 10* 11	Date paid
		£	£	£	£	£	£	£	£	£	£	£	
6 April to 5 May Month 1	1												
	2												
	3												
	4												
	Total												
6 May to 5 June Month 2	5												
	6												
	7												
	8												
	Total												
6 June to 5 July Month 3	9												
	10												
	11												
	12												
	13												
	Total												
6 July to 5 Aug Month 4	14												
	15												
	16												
	17												
	Total												
6 Aug to 5 Sept Month 5	18												
	19												
	20												
	21												
	Total												
6 Sept to 5 Oct Month 6	22												
	23												
	24												
	25												
	26												
	Total												
6 Oct to 5 Nov Month 7	27												
	28												
	29												
	30												
	Total												
6 Nov to 5 Dec Month 8	31												
	32												
	33												
	34												
	35												
	Total												
6 Dec to 5 Jan Month 9	36												
	37												
	38												
	39												
	Total												
6 Jan to 5 Feb Month 10	40												
	41												
	42												
	43												
	Total												
6 Feb to 5 Mar Month 11	44												
	45												
	46												
	47												
	Total												
6 Mar to 5 April Month 12	48												
	49												
	50												
	51												
	52												
	§												
	Total												

§ Complete this line if pay day falls on 5 April (in leap years 4 & 5 April)

Note The monthly NICs and SSP totals on this form may not be the same as the monthly totals for recovering SSP under the Percentage Threshold Scheme

This total should agree the NIC total on form P35 ▶ ◀ This total should agree the tax total on form P35

P32(1997)

Section 6

More Advanced PAYE Calculations

So far, we have looked at a simple PAYE calculation. Life would be wonderful if this was all there is to it. Unfortunately, there are a few more things we need to know if we are to operate real life payroll calculations.

In this section, we will:

- Take a more detailed look at tax codes
- See how to handle leavers and joiners
- See how to calculate wages when the employee has a K code.

Tax Codes

Tax Codes Suffixes

In Section 5, we said that a tax code represents the amount of money that an employee is allowed to earn free of income tax. The tax code is shown with the last digit removed (eg £4045 of tax free earnings is shown as 404). To complete the tax code, a letter from the alphabet is normally added.

Suffixes 'L', 'H', 'P', 'V' and 'T' are explained below.

- 'L' stands for the lower personal allowance. This is the single person's allowance for the particular tax year.
- 'H' stands for the higher personal allowance. This comprises the single personal allowance plus the married couple's allowance.
- 'P' stands for the personal allowance of someone over pension age.
- 'V' stands for the personal age allowance plus the married couple's age allowance.
- 'T' denotes a transitional allowance that must be reviewed individually by the Inland Revenue each year and either increased or decreased by issue of Form P6(T) (see page 38). 'T' codes are also issued where the employee does not want the suffix code to reveal their personal circumstances and, therefore, may appear for confidentiality purposes.

Suffixes streamline the operation of PAYE. Each year in the annual Budget, the Chancellor announces increases or decreases in personal allowances. These general increases or decreases are notified to employers by the Inland Revenue on Form P9X (see example on page 51) which arrives with the Employer's Annual Pack. These tell the employer to increase or decrease *all* employees' tax codes for which that suffix applies, eg increase 'L' suffix code by 28. This avoids the necessity for the Inland Revenue to issue a new notice of coding for every employee each year.

Tax Code Prefixes

Sometimes, tax codes have the *prefix* 'K' or 'D' before them; these warn the employer that special circumstances apply.

Form P9X(1997)

PAYE - *instructions to employers*

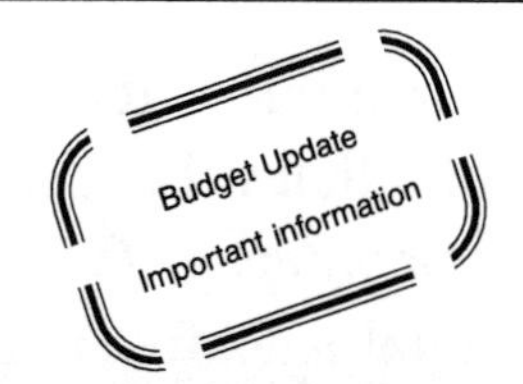

November 1996 Budget Proposals: What you must do

1 Forms P9(T) code changes to be operated from 6 April 1997

Form P9(T) is a Notice of Employee's Code to be operated from the 6 April next.

Notification of code changes may also be sent to you by list or on magnetic tape if you require this. Code changes notified on form P9(T) (or list or tape) will include **all** the changes announced in the Budget in November. Bulk notifications will be sent in February and early March.

Where you receive a code notification for any employee please follow the procedures outlined in card 2 of the CWG1(1997) enclosed with the Annual Pack.

2 Code changes where a P9(T) has not been received

Where you do not receive a code notification you should firstly carry forward the latest 1996-97 code. Where codes are carried forward from 1996-97, bear in mind the following

- if you received a P6 too late to use it for 1996-97, you should nevertheless carry forward the code shown on that P6
- do not carry forward any Week 1 or Month 1 markings from 1996-97.

You are required to amend PAYE codes you carry forward which have an L, H, P or V suffix and use the amended code from 6 April 1997. Amend these codes as follows:

INCREASE the following suffix codes

Suffix code L - increase by 28 (e.g. code 376L becomes 404L)
Suffix code H - increase by 36 (e.g. code 488H becomes 524H)
Suffix code P - increase by 31 (e.g. code 491P becomes 522P)
Suffix code V - increase by 44 (e.g. code 686V becomes 730V)

Please enter the amended code on the Deductions Working Sheet.

Step by step advice on how to carry out these changes is contained in card 2 of the CWG1(1997).

Do not change -

- a suffix T code or a prefix D or K code unless the Tax Office has sent you a notification on form P9(T) (or list or tape) (see **1**. above)
- any code where you have received a form P9(T) (or list or tape entry) - see card 2 of the CWG1(1997) for further information
- the code of any employee who leaves before, or on, 5 April 1997 (even where, because of 'lying time', the last wages payment is made on or after 5 April 1997).

3 New employees

Where a new employee

- is engaged between 6 April 1997 and 24 May 1997 **and**
- the date of leaving shown on his/her P45 is after 5 April 1996 **but before** 6 April 1997 **and**
- the code has an L, H, P or V suffix

you should amend the code in accordance with the instructions in paragraph **2** and enter the amended code at item 11 on part 3 of the form P45. You should operate the amended code from the date of commencement.

4 PAYE threshold and Emergency Code from 6 April 1997

The PAYE threshold (the specified amount of pay above which PAYE must be operated) is increased to £78.00 per week (£338 per month).

The code specified for emergency use is 404L. Refer to Cards 5 and 8 of the CWG1(1997) for futher information.

5 Tax Tables

New Taxable Pay Tables LR + B to D (April 1997 issue) are enclosed with the Annual Pack. Use these new tables from 6 April 1997. Once the new tables are in use please scrap Taxable Pay Tables (April 1996 issue). **Continue to use Pay Adjustment Tables A (1993 issue).**

For employers on the ADP mailing list who are responsible for their own reprogramming, amendments needed to the "Specification for PAYE Tax Table routines" were contained in "Notes on PAYE for Computer Users" Series 9 Number 7 which was issued in December 1996.

6 Other changes

All other changes which affect the operation of PAYE are incorporated in the forms and literature enclosed with this notice.

P9X(1997)

K Codes

K codes came into effect from 6 April 1993. Since that date, car scale charges have increased so that it is now common for individuals' taxable benefits to exceed their personal allowances. Generally, the Inland Revenue tax benefits in kind by reducing the individual's tax free personal allowance by the amount of the benefit (this is called 'coding out'). This enables the Revenue to collect tax on benefits throughout the tax year.

Prior to the introduction of K codes, benefits and personal allowances were not 'coded out'. This gave rise to an annual income tax charge which could not be collected until an assessment was issued some time after the end of the tax year. This caused more work for the Inland Revenue and employees were suddenly presented with a tax bill which they might not have anticipated. To avoid this problem, employees whose benefits exceed their personal allowances are now given a 'K' code.

K codes are not just for people with company cars; all benefits are taxable where employees earn over £8,500. Surprisingly, this tax threshold has remained at £8,500 since 1979. Each year, more and more employees are caught in the benefits trap which means that K codes are becoming increasingly common.

The K code consists of the prefix K followed by a number, eg K468. The number represents the *excess* value of the benefits in kind after deducting the employee's tax free allowances. This excess is converted into taxable pay and added to the employee's weekly or monthly earnings. This allows the Inland Revenue to deduct the full amount of tax on benefits from salary throughout the year.

K codes can cause excessive tax deductions if pay fluctuates from one month to another. The amount of tax to be deducted, therefore, is subject to a maximum restriction of 50% of gross pay. This is called the 'regulatory limit'. The Inland Revenue have decided that a deduction exceeding 50% could cause hardship. The employee does not escape the additional tax over 50% of pay. This will be collected either in a later month or by a tax demand after the end of the tax year. Employees subject to a K code suffered a drop in their routine take-home pay after April 1993.

D Codes

D codes are an instruction to deduct tax at 40%. No allowance is made for personal allowances or tax at the 20% or 23% rate bands. Tax is deducted at a straight 40% on the total gross earnings. This usually indicates that the employee has earnings from another source which already takes them into the higher rate of tax.

Other Codes

There are other special tax codes which denote the status of the employee. Examples include:

- 'OT' - this indicates that no allowances are due and that *all* the employee's pay is taxable.

- 'NT' - indicates that no tax is to be deducted from the employee's pay. This is an uncommon tax code. Here is an example of how this tax code could arise. A self-employed solicitor could be asked to sit on a professional body because of his or her professional status. Normally, payment for this work would be subject to PAYE. However, provided that the Inland Revenue agrees, the pay can be added to the solicitor's self-employed income and taxed under Schedule D.

- 'NI' - this indicates that the employee will have no tax liability. This would occur, for example, if the earnings weren't likely to exceed the single person's tax free allowances.

- 'BR' - stands for basic rate. This code instructs the employer to deduct tax from all earnings at 23%. You should not make any allowance for lower rate relief and, therefore, should not use the subtraction tables. Tax should be deducted at a straight 23% of total gross earnings.

- Emergency Tax Codes - the emergency tax code applies where an employee commences employment but is unable to provide the employer with a form P45. The emergency tax code is the equivalent of the single person's allowance for the year, ie £4045 for 1997/98; however, it is operated on a Week 1 or Month 1 basis (see below).

- Week 1/Month 1 Basis - this is an instruction to the employer to operate the tax code separately each week or month as if it were the first week or month of the tax year. Generally, PAYE operates on a cumulative basis, ie tax is calculated on the total pay to date with allowances being made for tax deducted in previous months. However, operating a Week 1 or Month 1 basis avoids the cumulative nature of PAYE. This generally means that the employee pays higher amounts of tax than usual. This type of tax collection is used where there is an under-deduction of tax part-way through the tax year. By applying a Month 1 or Week 1 basis, the taxpayer eliminates the underpayment over the remainder of the tax year.

What About Leavers and Joiners?

In our previous example, Bill Gates was already on the payroll on the first day of the tax year. How do we handle people who join or leave part-way through the year? This is easy provided we know:

- the employee's earnings so far this tax year
- the employee's tax deductions so far in this tax year
- the employee's tax code.

Providing we can enter these figures on the P11, we have sufficient information to continue to make tax deductions for the remainder of the tax year. This information is relayed from one employer to the next on a P45 form.

Dealing with Leavers

Let's see how we would prepare a P45 if Bill Gates had left Mainbrew on 5 June. In the example on page 41, we completed Bill Gates' wage calculation up until 5 June. As a reminder, the wage calculation is reproduced below.

Mainbrew Ltd

123/M4567

Employee's surname *in CAPITALS* Gates First two forenames William John

National Insurance no. ZX 00 11 22 B | Date of Birth *in figures* 17 03 44 | Works no. etc 14 | Date of starting

Tax code † 524H | Amended code † | Wk/Mth in which | Date of leaving Day Month Year

PAYE Income Tax

For guidance on completing this form see CWG1 'Employer's Quick Guide to Pay As You Earn and National Insurance Contributions'

- *Card 10 for general completion*
- *Card 12 specifically for K codes*
- *Cards 11 and 12 for examples using suffix and K codes*

Month no	Week no	Pay in the week or month including Statutory Sick Pay/Statutory Maternity Pay 2 £	Total pay to date 3 £	Total free pay to date (Table A) 4a £	K codes: Total 'additional pay' to date (Table A) 4b £	Total taxable pay to date i.e. column 3 *minus* column 4a **or** column 3 *plus* column 4b 5 £	Total tax due to date as shown by Taxable Pay Tables 6 £	K codes only: Tax due at end of current period Mark refunds 'R' 6a £	K codes only: Regulatory limit i.e. 50% of column 2 entry 6b £	Tax deducted or refunded in the week or month. Mark refunds 'R' 7 £	K codes only: Tax not deducted owing to the Regulatory limit 8 £	For employer's use
	1											
	2											
	3											
1	4	1100 00	1100 00	437 42		662 58	142 01			142 01		
	5											
	6											
	7											
2	8	1200 00	2300 00	874 84		1425 16	307 25			165 24		
	9											
	10											
	11											
	12											
3	13											

We can use the information on the P11 to complete Bill Gates' P45 as follows.

Inland Revenue

Details of employee leaving work
Copy for Tax Office

P45 Part 1

1 PAYE Reference	District number: 123	Reference number: M4567
2 Employee's National Insurance number	ZX 00 11 22 B	
3 Surname (in capitals)	Gates	(Mr Mrs Miss Ms) Mr
First name(s) (in capitals)	William John	
4 Leaving date (in figures)	Day 05 Month 06 Year 19 97	
5 Tax Code at leaving date. *If Week 1 or Month 1 basis applies, write 'X' in the box marked Week 1 or Month 1*	Code 524H	Week 1 or Month 1
6 Last entries on *Deductions Working Sheet* (P11) ***Complete only if Tax Code is cumulative.*** *Make no entry here if Week 1 or Month 1 basis applies. Go to item 7.*	Week or month number	Week / Month. 2
	Total pay to date	£ 2300 00 p
	Total tax to date	£ 307 25 p
7 This employment pay and tax. *No entry needed if Tax code is cumulative and amounts are same as item 6 entry.*	Total pay in this employment	£ p
	Total tax in this employment	£ p
8 Works number Payroll number	14	9 Department or branch if any: N/A
10 Employee's private address and Postcode	19 Acacia Avenue Fareham Hants Po16 3ZX	

11 I certify that the details entered above in items 1 to 9 are correct

Employer's name, address and Postcode	Mainbrew Ltd Wallop Road Wallop Hants Po16 4DQ
Date	5 June 1997

To the employer

- Complete this form following the 'Employee leaving' instructions in the *Employer's Basic Guide to PAYE* (P8). Make sure the details are clear on all four parts of this form. Make sure your name and address is shown on Parts 1 and lA.
- Detach Part 1 and send it to your Tax Office immediately.
- Hand Parts 1 A, 2 and 3 (unseparated) to your employee when he or she leaves.
- If the employee has died, write 'D' in this box and send all four parts of this form (unseparated) to your Tax Office immediately.

P45(1996)

For Tax Office use

CCO 2/95

How the P45 System Works

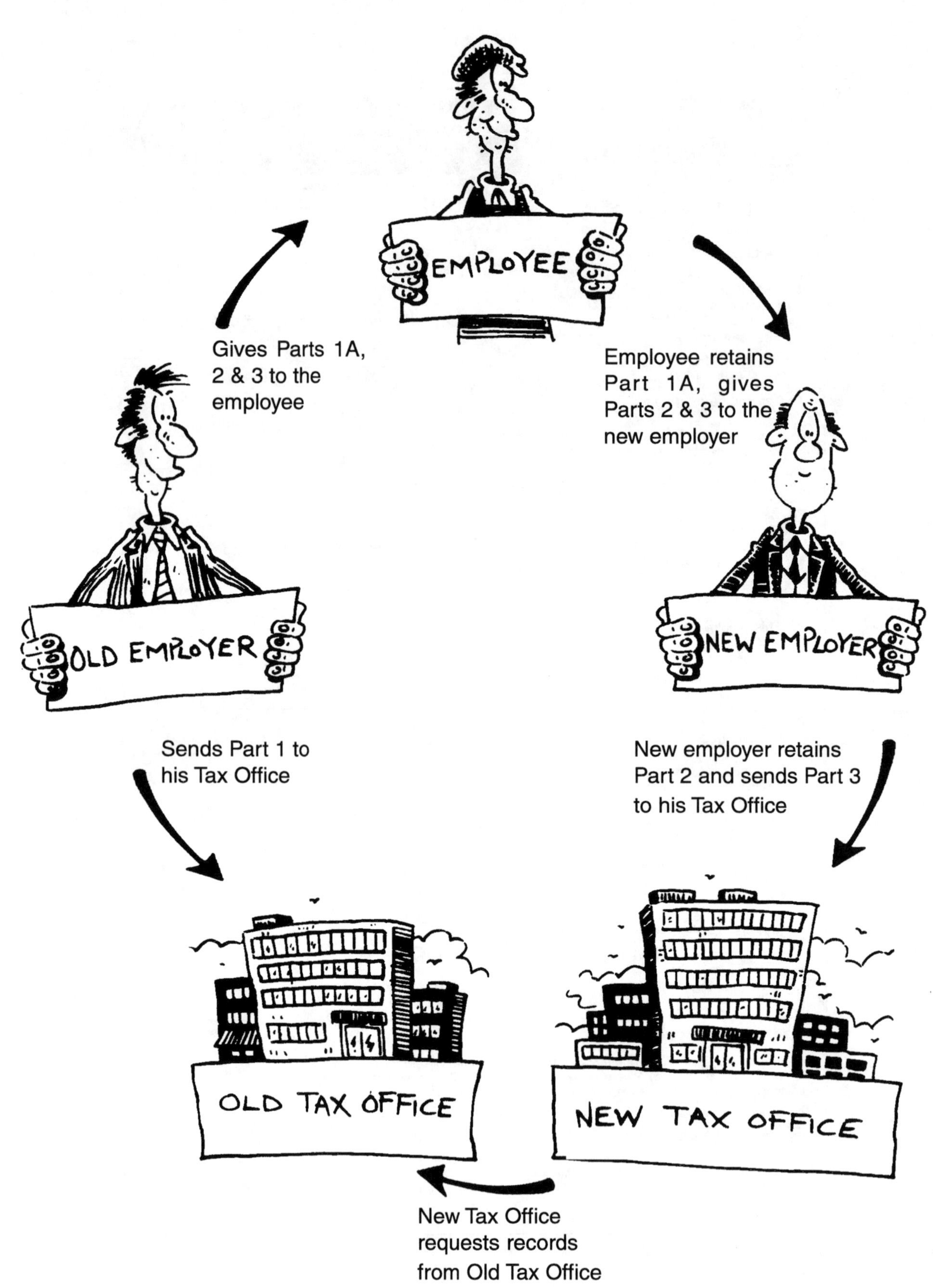
EMPLOYEE
Gives Parts 1A, 2 & 3 to the employee
Employee retains Part 1A, gives Parts 2 & 3 to the new employer
OLD EMPLOYER
NEW EMPLOYER
Sends Part 1 to his Tax Office
New employer retains Part 2 and sends Part 3 to his Tax Office
OLD TAX OFFICE
NEW TAX OFFICE
New Tax Office requests records from Old Tax Office

Note that the P45 includes the three key figures which the next employer needs to pick up the payroll calculation for the current tax year, viz:

- Earnings to date in this tax year
- Deductions to date in this tax year
- The employee's tax code.

The P45 form has four pages, these are numbered parts 1, 1A, 2 and 3.

When the P45 is complete, send Part 1 to your tax office straightaway. Give Parts 1A, 2 and 3 to the employee when he/she leaves. More detailed instructions for dealing with a P45 are contained in Card 7 of the Employer's Quick Guide to PAYE and NICs, CWG1 (1997). A diagram showing how the P45 is used by the old and new employers and tax offices is shown on page 56.

Dealing with Joiners

A new employee will normally arrive with Parts 1A, 2 and 3 of his P45. Give Part 1A back to the employee to keep. Part 3 should be sent to the tax office. Retain Part 2 for your own records.

The information given on a P45 is enough to start a new P11 deductions working sheet. Let's use the P45 we have already prepared. We will assume that Bill Gates starts a new job with Technobrew on 1 August.

Example

Bill Gates left his old company, Mainbrew, to take up a position with a new company, Technobrew. For the purposes of our example, we will use the P45 shown on page 55.

We will assume that Bill Gates started his new employment on 1 August after having a couple of months off work. His first pay day will be 31 August.

Step 1 When Bill Gates presents his form P45, the new employer should check whether the tax deductions made by the previous employer were correct. This is done by entering the 'Total Pay to Date' given on the P45 in column 3 on the P11 immediately above the line where the first deduction in the new employment is to be made (see example on page 59).

Contd

Example (Contd)

Use the Tax Tables relating to the date when Bill Gates left his previous job to complete columns 4a, 5 and 6. The reason for this is to check that the previous pay and tax figures were correctly computed. If you do not agree the total tax as entered in column 6, you should enter the total tax which you calculate to have been due at item 12 on the P45 Part 3. If you discover a mistake, enter the ***incorrect*** amounts of 'total pay to date' and 'total tax to date' figures on your P11 deductions working sheet. Any error made by the previous employer will be automatically corrected when you make your first tax calculation of the new employment.

Step 2 You can see in the example on page 59 that we have checked the previous entries on the Form P45 and found them to be correct. They have been entered onto the line immediately above that for the first pay day (which is 31 August). We have entered £2300 in column 3 which is the total gross pay to 5 June. We then looked up the Pay Adjustment Tables (Tables A) at Month 2 and found the free pay on code 524H to be £874.84. This was entered in column 4a. We also entered £1425.16 in column 5; it is the total pay to date less total free pay to date (£2300 - £874.84). We then referred to our Taxable Pay Tables at Month 2 and found that Table B applies. We then checked the total tax due and computed it to be £307.25 (remembering to take account of the amount to be subtracted for the lower rate band). We made a note in the final column (P45) as a reminder that these were the P45 figures supplied to us.

Step 3 Assume Bill Gates is paid £1200 on 31 August (after a short break in employment). In column 3 we have added his August pay to the existing total pay to date figure to give us a new total pay to date figure of £3500.

Step 4 We now need to compute the total free pay applicable to Month 5. If you have a set of Pay Adjustment Tables (Table A), look up Month 5. You will see that the free pay based on the tax code of 524 is £2187.10. This is entered in column 4a.

Step 5 In column 5, enter the total taxable pay to date which is arrived at by deducting the total free pay in column 4a from the total pay to date in column 3 (£3500 - £2187.10). This gives us a figure of £1312.90.

Contd

Example

Technobrew

Employee's surname *in CAPITALS* Gates	First two forenames William John	
National Insurance no. ZX 00 11 22 B	Date of Birth *in figures* 17 03 44	Works no. etc None

Date of starting: Day | Month | Year

Date of leaving: Day | Month | Year

Tax code †	Amended code †
524H	Wk/Mth in which applied

PAYE Income Tax

For guidance on completing this form see CWG1 'Employer's Quick Guide to Pay Aa You Earn and National Insurance Contributions'

- *Card 10 for general completion*
- *Card 12 specifically for K codes*
- *Cards 11 and 12 for examples using suffix and K codes*

Month no	Week no	2 Pay in the week or month including Statutory Sick Pay/Statutory Maternity Pay £	3 Total pay to date £	4a Total free pay to date (Table A) £	K codes: 4b Total 'additional pay' to date (Table A) £	5 Total taxable pay to date i.e. column 3 *minus* column 4a **or** column 3 *plus* column 4b £	6 Total tax due to date as shown by Taxable Pay Tables £	K codes only: 6a Tax due at end of current period Mark refunds 'R' £	K codes only: 6b Regulatory limit i.e. 50% of column 2 entry £	7 Tax deducted or refunded in the week or month. Mark refunds 'R' £	K codes only: 8 Tax not deducted owing to the Regulatory limit £	For employer's use
	1											
	2											
	3											
1	4											
	5											
	6											
	7											
2	8											
	9											
	10											
	11											
	12											
3	13											
	14											
	15											
	16											
4	17											
	18											
	19											
	20		2300 00	874 84		1425 16	307 25					P45
5	21	1200 00	3500 00	2187 10		1312 90	262 40			44 85		R
	22											
	23											
	24											
	25											
6	26	2000 00	5500 00	2624 52		2875 48	599 75			337 35		
	27											
	28											
	29											
7	30											

Step 3 Page 58

Steps 1 & 2 Pages 57-58

Step 4 Page 58

Step 5 Page 58

Step 6 Page 60

Step 7 Page 60

Step 8 Pages 60-61

Example (Contd)

Step 6 The next stage in the calculation is to refer to the Taxable Pay Tables LR + B to D. As before, our starting point is the table on page 184 which tells us which tax table to use. We look up Month 5 which directs us to Table LR because the pay of £1312.90 does not exceed £1709. We can look up the tax on £1312 and see that the tax due is £262.40. Table LR taxes the income at 20% - there is no lower rate adjustment of the kind seen on table B.

Step 7 Work out the total tax payable by taking the 'total tax due to date' of £262.40 from the figure of tax already deducted which is shown on our Form P45 as £307.25. From this we can see that the total tax due at Month 5 produces a refund of £44.85 to the employee. We would, therefore, enter £44.85 in column 7 and would mark this refund with an 'R' in the final column to make it clear that this was a tax refund.

Here is the reason for the refund. Bill Gates has not worked in Months 3 and 4. This means that he has two months' unused allowances. Since PAYE is cumulative, when he is paid in Month 5 he will have his total tax free allowances (ie 5/12ths) available to set against total pay at that date. Often where there is a gap between employments, this will produce a refund on the first pay day in the new employment. Refer to page 67 for further information regarding tax refunds.

Step 8 To continue our computation, in Month 6 Bill Gates was paid £2000 which is entered into column 2 of the form P11. In column 3 of the form P11, we calculate the total pay to date which is £5500 (£3500 + £2000). Look up the total free pay for Month 6 from the Pay Adjustment Tables and enter the value in column 4a. The total free pay is £2624.52.

We enter the total taxable pay in column 5 which is arrived at by taking the total free pay to date of £2624.52 from total pay to date of £5500. This gives us total taxable pay of £2875.48.

We then need to refer to the taxable pay tables, first checking which table relates to the level of pay at Month 6. Turn to the table on page 184 and we can see by reading across from Month 6 that the total pay (in Month 6) exceeds £2050 but does not exceed £13050. We should, therefore, use Table B.

Contd

Example (Contd)

Turn to Table B on page 186 and look up the total tax due on £2875. To start with, look up the tax on £2800 which gives us tax of £644.00. To this, we have to add tax on £75 which is given in the shaded table on the same page. Tax on £75 amounts to £17.25. This means that Bill Gates would pay £661.25 of tax if all his earnings were taxed at 23%.

However, the first £4100 of income is only taxed at 20%. This means that we have to subtract the amounts shown in the Table B Subtraction Tables for Month 6 (see page 187) which is £61.50. This gives a total cumulative year to date tax owed of £599.75. If we subtract total tax paid to date (£262.40) from total tax due to date (£599.75), we get tax due this month of £337.35 which is entered in column 7.

How to Deal With an Employee Without a P45

Sometimes, a new employee arrives without a P45. This could be for a variety of reasons. For example, he could have:

- been unemployed
- been previously self employed
- lost his P45
- previously worked abroad.

If a new employee arrives without a P45, ask him why he doesn't have one. If the old employer didn't give the leaver a P45, get your new employee to request one. The old employer cannot refuse because there is a statutory obligation on all employers to provide a P45 on cessation of employment.

If the previous employer did provide a P45 which the employee subsequently lost then the previous employer cannot issue a duplicate since this is not allowed by law. This is designed to prevent fraud. In this instance, the employee receives the same treatment as if he had never been given a P45. You will need to give him a P46.

If the employee arrives with a P45 relating to an earlier tax year (this could occur where an employee took a long time to find a new job), don't ask for a P45 from the old employer (it wouldn't be of any relevance to this tax year anyway).

Employees who were previously self employed, or who were working abroad, will not have a P45 since they had no UK employer who is in a position to issue a P45. In this instance, ask them to complete a P46. The instructions for using P46s follow shortly.

Where an employee was previously claiming unemployment benefit, he should immediately advise the Unemployment Benefit Office that he wishes to cease claiming. If the employee provided the Unemployment Benefit Office with details of pay and tax on a form P45 when he commenced claiming then the Unemployment Benefit Office will issue a form P45U to the employee which is treated exactly as a form P45.

How to Use a Form P46

Where the employee arrives without a form P45, the employer must complete a form P46. An example is shown on page 63. Form P46 is used to provide information to the Inland Revenue so that they can assess the employee's circumstances and issue the correct tax code.

As you will see on the front of form P46 on page 63, there are three statements. These are Statement A, Statement B and Statement C. The tax code to be operated will depend on whether the employee signs:

- Statement A
- Statement B
- Statement C
- None of them.

Statement A

Statement A shows that this is the employee's first regular job since leaving full-time education. It also states that the employee has not claimed unemployed benefit or income support. If the employee signs this statement, and the anticipated level of pay is more than the National Insurance threshold, then a completed form P46 should be sent to the Inland Revenue immediately. Prepare a deductions working sheet (P11) and deduct tax on the cumulative basis using the emergency code which is currently 404L.

PAYE Employer's notice to Tax Office — P46

Use this form to tell the Tax Office about
- employees who do not have a form P45 or
- employees previously paid below the PAYE threshold.

To be completed by the employee
Read each statement below carefully. Tick **each one** that applies to you. If none of them apply, do not sign the statement. Complete the lower part of this form.

√

Statement A
This is my first regular job since leaving full-time education. I have not claimed Jobseekers Allowance, or income support paid because of unemployment since then. ☐

Statement B
This is my only or main job. ☐

Statement C
I receive a pension as well as the income from this job. ☐

I confirm I have ticked the statements that apply to me.

Signed ____________________ Date __________

To be completed by the employer

Employer's name ☐

Employer's address ☐ ☐

Postcode

Employer's PAYE reference (*District no.* / *Reference*) ☐

Date this form was completed (*Day* / *Month* / *Year*) ☐ ☐ ☐

P46(1996) CCO 8/96

Employee's details ***- to be entered by the employer***

National Insurance number (*Letters* / *Numbers* / *Numbers* / *Numbers* / *Letter*) ☐ ☐ ☐ ☐ ☐

Surname including title Mr/Mrs/Miss/Ms (*Title* / *Surname*) ☐

First name(s) ☐

Home Address ☐ ☐

Postcode

Date of birth (in figures) (*Day* / *Month* / *Year*) ☐ ☐ ☐

Put 'M' for male of 'F' for female in box ☐

Works or payroll number, *if any* ☐

Branch or department, *if any* ☐

Job title ☐

Date employment started ☐ ☐ ☐

Coding information ***to be completed by employer***

Existing employee now above PAYE threshold ☐
enter X in box if this applies

New employee who has signed statement *enter letter here* ☐

New employee who has not signed a statement ☐

Code operated for this employee ☐

Enter X in box if code operated on week 1/month 1 basis ☐

Employee *if you wish you can detach this part and send it to the Tax Office yourself. Ask your employer for the Tax Office's address.*

Your employer's PAYE reference ☐

Your National Insurance number (*Letters* / *Numbers* / *Numbers* / *Numbers* / *Letter*) ☐ ☐ ☐ ☐ ☐

Completing this form will help your employer and the Tax Office to give you a correct PAYE code. Without it you pay too much or too little tax.
Please list below in date order all the jobs you have had and any periods when you were out of work during the last **twelve months**. Please do not leave any gaps between the periods. If you were claiming benefit while you were out of work please show this in the space provided.

Under **Additional information** give the following details
- your employer's name and address if you were employed
- your business name and address if you were self-employed
- the type of benefit you claimed while out of work
- what you were doing if you were not working and not claiming benefit, for example, in full time education.

Use a separate sheet if there is not enough space on this slip.

Dates		*Tick one box for each period*				
From	To	Employed	Self employed	Claiming benefit	Not working	Additional information
______	______	☐	☐	☐	☐	______________
______	______	☐	☐	☐	☐	______________
______	______	☐	☐	☐	☐	______________

P46(Slip)

Copy notice For DSS use

P46

Use this form to tell the DSS about

- employees who do not have a form P45 or
- employees previously paid below the PAYE threshold.

Employee's details - ***to be entered by the employer***

National Insurance number — *Letters* | *Numbers* | *Numbers* | *Numbers* | *Letter*

Surname including title Mr/Mrs/Miss/Ms
Title *Surname*

First name(s)

Home Address

Postcode

Date of birth (in figures) — *Day* *Month* *Year*

Put 'M' for male of 'F' for female in box

Works or payroll number, *if any*

Branch or department, *if any*

Job title

Date employment started — *Day* *Month* *Year*

To be completed by the employer

Employer's name

Employer's address

Postcode

Employer's PAYE reference — *District no.* *Reference*

Date this form was completed — *Day* *Month* *Year*

If the projected annual pay is less than the PAYE threshold but more than the NIC lower earnings limit, you should keep the completed P46 and prepare a deductions working sheet. You will obviously have no PAYE to deduct but you should record national insurance contributions on form P11. Enter 'NI' in the tax code space.

If the pay is less than the PAYE threshold and less than the NIC lower earnings limit, you should simply keep the completed form P46. There is no need to prepare a deductions working sheet as the employee will not be liable to tax or national insurance. You should, however, record the employee's name and address and the amount of pay in each week or month. You should be careful if the pay increases as it could exceed the national insurance lower earnings limit or the PAYE threshold at a later date. You will then need to start deducting tax and national insurance.

Statement B

If the employee signs Statement B, they have stated that this is their only or main job. Your course of action will depend on the level of employee earnings as follows.

If the level of pay is above the NI threshold and high enough to warrant income tax deductions under PAYE, send form P46 to the Inland Revenue immediately. Prepare a deductions working sheet (P11) and deduct national insurance and income tax on either a Week 1 or Month 1 basis using the emergency code which is currently 404L. Remember that, by operating the Week 1 or Month 1 basis, allowances are not given cumulatively.

If the total pay in the week or month is more than the national insurance lower earnings limit but too small to attract PAYE deductions, you should keep form P46 and prepare a deductions working sheet. You should enter 'NI' in the tax code space and record only national insurance. You should keep a record of the employee's name and address and the amount of pay in each week or month.

Where the total pay is too low to attract PAYE or national insurance contributions, simply keep the completed form P46. There is no need to prepare a deductions working sheet as the pay will not be liable to tax or national insurance. You should, however, record the employee's name and address and the amount of pay in each week or month. Again, remember to review the position if the pay increases, in case national insurance or PAYE becomes due.

Statement C

Pensioners work too!

Statement C applies to people who are employed but also draw a pension. In the old days, a person could sign Statement B quite truthfully when he received both an income and a pension. Unfortunately, the tax office then took this to mean that all of his income came from his job. This meant that he received personal allowances on both his pension *and* his job. Later in the year, the truth would become apparent so the employee then received a surprise tax bill based on his combined pension/job earnings. Statement C prevents this happening.

No Statement Signed

Where the employee hasn't signed any Statement, you can assume that the employee has more than one job. If the pay is over £1 per week or £4 per month then the completed form P46 must be sent to the Inland Revenue immediately. You should prepare a deductions working sheet (P11) and tax should be deducted using code BR (ie deduct tax at 23% on the whole of the earnings).

Importance of Form P46

Form P46 is an important document. It should be completed for every employee who does not provide a form P45, *irrespective of the level of their earnings*. Employers often fail to complete a form P46 for casual employees who are paid below the tax and national insurance threshold. If the Inland Revenue conduct a PAYE compliance visit, they will want to see the completed form P46 for every employee, irrespective of earnings. If the employer is unable to provide these forms, the Inland Revenue will assume that all employees have jobs elsewhere which would utilise their personal allowances. The Inland Revenue would then deem *all* wages paid to be subject to tax and national insurance contributions (irrespective of their level). The employer can be held responsible for payment of these tax and national insurance contributions not only for the year in which P46s have not been completed, but for up to six years previously, unless the employer can prove that the same circumstances did not apply.

This is why it is important to complete a form P46 for every employee who does not provide a form P45.

Dealing with Tax Refunds on Change of Employment

We have mentioned before that PAYE is deducted on a cumulative basis. This means that an employee may be entitled to a refund of tax on joining a new employer. This arises because there will be periods when the employee attracts tax free allowances at a time when he has no income to offset these allowances. In the past, you needed authorisation from the Inland Revenue to refund amounts exceeding £200. This is no longer the case. You can refund the amount due to the employee direct. If a refund is given, you should clearly mark this on the deductions working sheet form P11 by putting an 'R' in column 7.

There are circumstances in which you cannot make a refund to an employee. These are:

- If you are using a tax code on a Week 1 or Month 1 basis including cases where you are using the emergency code
- If you are using code NT for the employee
- If you are using a code that starts with D
- If the employee is involved in a trade dispute.

How to Operate K Codes

K Codes operate in a similar way to normal suffix codes except that they ***add*** taxable pay instead of ***deducting*** tax free pay. To illustrate the point, let's have a look at Sally's wages.

Example

Sally has a company car. She has a tax code of K426. The appropriate P11 is shown on page 69.

Step 1 Assume Sally is paid £1100 in month 1. Columns 2 and 3 are the same as before. Instead of deducting 'tax free' pay in column 4a, we now add 'additional pay' in column 4b. The amount of additional pay is found from the pay adjustment tables for month 1 as before (use K code 426).

Step 2 The sum of the normal pay and the 'additional pay' is entered in column 5, ie £1100 + £355.75 = £1455.75.

Contd

Example (Contd)

Step 3 Tax on £1455.75 falls within Table B of the taxable pay tables. Tax due is calculated as:

	£
Tax on £1400	322.00
Tax on £55	12.65
	334.65
Less lower rate relief	10.25
Tax Payable	324.40

Step 4 The maximum amount that may be deducted in any month is 50% of the pay of that month. This is a safeguard to prevent unusual circumstances taking all the employee's pay for that month! This is called the 'regulatory' limit, it is entered in column 6b. For Sally, the regulatory limit is £550 for Month 1 (ie half of £1100).

Step 5 Sally's tax deduction is the lesser amount of columns 6a and 6b. In our example, this amounts to £324.40 which is the sum entered in column 7. We will deduct £324.40 from this Month 1 pay to cover income tax.

Step 6 Month 2 is calculated in a similar way to Month 1. If Sally is paid £1200 in Month 2, her cumulative pay will amount to £2300 which is entered in column 3.

Step 7 We can look up the additional pay for K426 in the pay adjustment tables for Month 2, this amounts to £711.50.

Step 8 We now *add* columns 3 and 4b to produce Month 2 taxable income which is £3011.50.

Step 9 Tax on £3011.50 for Month 2 falls within Table B of the taxable pay tables. Tax for this month would amount to:

	£
Tax on £3000	690.00
Tax on £11	2.53
	692.53
Less lower rate relief	20.50
Tax for month 2	672.03

Contd

Deductions Working Sheet P11 Year to 5 April 19__

forenames Sally

Works no. etc 12

Date of starting *in figures*		
Day	Month	Year

Date of leaving *in figures*		
Day	Month	Year

National Insurance contributions

For guidance on National Insurance and the completion of columns 1a to 1h see CWG1 'Employer's Quick Guide to Pay As You Earn and National Insurance Contributions' - card 9

For guidance on Statutory Sick Pay figures see leaflet CA30

For guidance on Statutory Maternity Pay figures see leaflet CA29

or contact the Employer's Help Line - telephone number is in the CWG1

At the top of each section in the NI Tables there is a letter, for examp *or E.* Copy that letter from the Table you use to the box bottom left o overleaf. If the employee's circumstances change part way through change as well. Record all letters with separate totals for each table Remember to record under letter Y any Class 1a on the last line of th

See the CWG1 card 11 for further information and examples

Insurance Contributions'

Earnings recorded in column 1a should not exceed the Upper Earnings Limit

For employer's use	Earnings on which employee's contributions payable *Whole pounds only* 1a £	Total of employee's and employer's contributions payable 1b £	Employee's contribution payable 1c £	Earnings on which employee's contributions at contracted-out rate payable included in col. 1a *Whole pounds only* 1d £	Em con con rate colu 1e	**K codes only** Tax due at end of current period Mark refunds 'R' 6a £	**K codes only** Regulatory limit i.e. 50% of column 2 entry 6b £	Tax deducted or refunded in the week or month. Mark refunds 'R' 7 £	**K codes only** Tax not deducted owing to the Regulatory limit 8 £	For employer's use
						Step 3 Page 68	Step 4 Page 68	Step 5 Page 68		
						324 40	550 00	324 40		
						347 63	600 00	347 63		
						Step 10 Page 71		Step 11 Page 71		
	Total c/fwd	Total c/fwd	Total c/fwd	Total c/fwd	T					

† If amended cross out previous code.

Ø If any week/month the amount in column 4a is more than the amount in column 3, leave column 5 blank.

P11(1997)

Employee's surname *in CAPITALS*	First two forenames

National Insurance no.	Date of birth *in figures* Day Month Year	Works no. etc	Date of starting *in figures* Day Month Year
			Date of leaving *in figures* Day Month Year

Tax code †	Amended code †				
	Wk/Mth in which applied				

ne Tax

Total pay to date 3	Total free pay to date (Table A) 4a	**K codes only** Total 'additional pay' to date (Table A) 4b	Total taxable pay to date i.e. column 3 *minus* column 4a **or** column 3 *plus* column 4b 5	Total tax due to date as shown by Taxable Pay Tables 6	**K codes only** Tax due at end of current period Mark refunds 'R' 6a	**K codes only** Regulatory limit i.e. 50% of column 2 entry 6b	Tax deducted or refunded in the week or month. Mark refunds 'R' 7	**K codes only** Tax not deducted owing to the Regulatory limit 8	For employer's use
£	£	£	£	£	£	£	£	£	

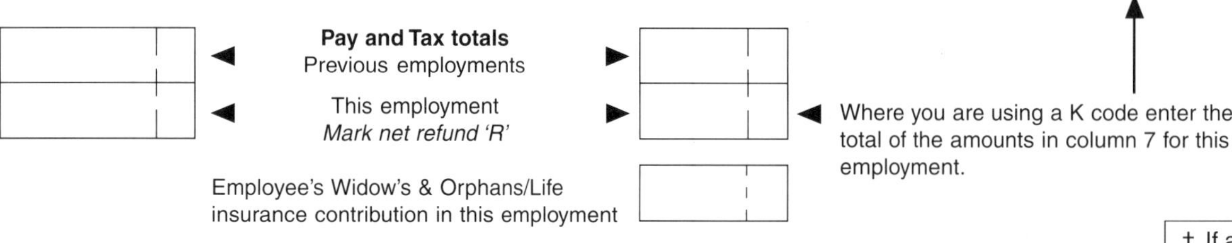

Pay and Tax totals
Previous employments

This employment
Mark net refund 'R'

Employee's Widow's & Orphans/Life insurance contribution in this employment

Where you are using a K code enter the total of the amounts in column 7 for this employment.

† If amended cross out previous code.

§ Complete this line if pay day falls on 5 April (in leap years 4 & 5 April).

ars after the end of the year to which it relates, or longer if you are asked to so so.

Example (Contd)

Step 10 Subtract the value in column 6 for Month 2 from the value in column 6 for Month 1 (£672.03 - £324.40) and put the result £347.63 in column 6a.

Step 11 The tax to be deducted from Sally's salary is the lower of the regulatory limit (£600) and the value in column 6a (£347.63). We enter £347.63 in column 7.

Important Note: The 'additional pay' added to pay for PAYE purposes has no effect on either the employee's or the employer's liability for National Insurance contributions.

Exercise 2

Calculate Sally's take home pay for June, July and August as follows:

Pay on 30 June	£1400
Pay on 31 July	£1250
Pay on 31 August	£1500

In case you don't have access to a full set of Taxable Pay tables, you may find the following useful:

MONTH	**TABLE A** Code K426 Pay Adjustment
	£
1	355.75
2	711.50
3	1067.25
4	1423.00
5	1778.75

Tables LR and B to D are to be found between pages 184 and 189 of this workbook. Use these to work out the tax due.

Check your answer with page 199.

Dealing with Casual Employees

The PAYE procedures for dealing with casual employees apply generally in the same way as they do for other employees. However, there are different rules for employees who are going to work for you for one week or less.

In these circumstances, there is no need to prepare a form P46. First establish whether the pay in the week is sufficient to attract PAYE. If it is, you must ask the employee whether they have any other employment. If they have other employment, you must prepare a deductions working sheet (P11) and deduct tax using tax code BR (ie at basic rate). If the employee does not have other employment, you should prepare a deductions working sheet and deduct tax on a Week 1/Month 1 basis using the emergency code.

If the total pay in the week is insufficient to attract PAYE but more than the national insurance lower earnings limit, prepare a deductions working sheet. You should enter 'NI' in the tax code space and record only national insurance contributions. Make a note of the employee's name and address and the amount of pay in each week.

If the pay in the week is less than the national insurance lower earnings limit, there is no need to prepare a deductions working sheet but you should, of course, still record the employee's name, address and the amount of pay.

Casual Labour

Payment Methods and Procedures

Your payroll department will work more efficiently if:

- All employees are paid monthly instead of weekly (because there are only 12 wages calculation a year instead of 52)
- All wages and salaries are paid by Electronic Funds Transfer. This avoids handling cash, which is inefficient and time consuming.

However, these arrangements may not suit everyone. Employees who either don't have bank accounts or find it difficult to reach banks during banks' normal opening hours will prefer weekly cash payments. The Wages Act 1986 repealed employees' rights to be paid in cash. The method of payment is now a contractual matter between the employer and the employee. The payment method will normally be documented in the employee's Contract of Employment.

Let's have a look at some methods of paying wages.

Payment by Cash

Payment by cash involves a great deal of administrative work, here are the steps:

- First the gross wage has to be calculated. If the wage includes bonus or overtime then the employee's manager should authorise the additional payment (which should be charged to his departmental budget).
- The payroll administrator then calculates statutory and voluntary deductions from the gross wage. This leaves a net wage to be paid to the employee.

- To minimise the amount of cash handling, the payroll office may round wages up to the nearest whole pound, or nearest whole five pounds. This reduces the need to handle coins. Roundings are carried forward from one month to the next and adjusted in the next wage calculation.

- Money has to be withdrawn from the bank in denominations necessary to make up each individual's pay packet. This is called a 'cash analysis'. It can either be calculated by hand or by a computerised payroll program.

- Cash has to be collected from the bank. This can be done by the firm's own staff or cash can be collected by a security carrier.

- The notes and coins are then put into wages packets, with the appropriate wages slip. This has to be done in such a way that the employee can check the contents without breaking the seal. This is obviously a huge time waster. From an audit point of view, you need to make sure that the cash taken from the bank for wages exactly balances the cash put into the wage packets.

- Wages are then distributed around the factory, office or site. Obviously, some people won't be present because of sickness or holidays. Others may be working off-site or at remote locations on the day that the payment is made. This involves further delay and security measures to ensure that the cash is stored safely until the employees can be given their pay.

- Naturally, each employee must sign for their wages otherwise a corrupt wages administrator could create an artifical pay packet as a means of fraud.

Payment by cash offers the greatest opportunity for fraud, mistake, errors and omissions. Some businesses will minimise the problem by subcontracting the activity to an outside security company. However, the best way to improve efficiency is to eliminate cash. This entails payment by cheque or electronic funds transfer.

Payment by Cheque

Payment by cheque is easier for the payroll office than payment by cash. However, it may create problems for the employee. Each employee has to find time to pay the cheque into the bank, wait for up to three working days for the cheque to clear and then withdraw cash from the bank.

Normally the employer will issue a cheque, crossed 'Account Payee', which ensures that the money can only be paid into a bank or building society. This makes cheque payment much more secure. Automated cheque runs can make cheques easier to produce. However, if more than ten employees are involved, you could probably save time by using electronic fund transfer.

The person calculating the wages should *never* sign the cheques. Cheques must be signed by the manager or supervisor who is responsible for overseeing wage payments.

Electronic Fund Transfer

The easiest and most convenient means of paying wages is undoubtedly by electronic fund transfer. Most banks can arrange electronic fund transfer. The following notes are based on the NatWest 'Autopay' service which is suitable for businesses employing up to 200 people.

Electronic funds transfer (EFT) has the following advantages:

- No special equipment is needed other than an ordinary personal computer and a modem.

- No special skill is needed - the data used by the system is entered on a form looking like any other administrative form.

- The system is secure in so far as no cash changes hands.

- EFT should produce a saving in bank charges, administrative costs and stationery.

- The system is flexible, all information is stored on the bank's database which is easy to update.

- The system is versatile. For example, an employee could receive two payments on one day. This could occur where he had both a salary and an expenses reimbursement due to him.

- Administrative effort is reduced. This should make payment much quicker, particularly where wages are calculated on a computerised payroll. The payroll program can be used to set up the EFT transfer over the telephone line.

How Do I Use EFT?

You will need to come to an agreement with a bank that operates an EFT service. This doesn't have to be your own bank although it will obviously be easier if you can use your own bank and conduct all business through your own branch. There is sufficient flexibility in the banking system to allow you to pay people via another bank should the need arise. This could be useful where an employee is based abroad or in a remote UK location where your own bank doesn't have a branch.

You will need to sign a contract with the bank. This contract will establish the mandate, set the bank's charges, and supply details like employees' names and bank details, security codes and, of course, details of the employer's bank account from which payment is to be made.

Although you can pay the wages by submitting a written request to your bank, this would destroy two of the main advantages which are speed and convenience. It makes much more sense to use software provided by the bank which enables you to transmit the payment data over a modem attached to your own computer. You will need to enter security codes which ensure that the transmission cannot be used fraudulently. The resulting payment will be debited to your account on the day of transmission and credited to your employees' accounts two working days later.

BACS

If you have over 200 employees, you may choose to make payment via the 'Bankers Automated Clearing System' (BACS). BACS payments are not, of course, restricted to salaries. Most large organisations use BACS to pay a wide range of invoices. BACS transactions take place on the specified payment day, this means that there is no loss of interest to the parties to the transaction. This can, of course, be a significant consideration when a large salaries payment is made. Payment by BACS can be arranged via your own bank.

Internal Check and Control of Wage Payments

In many organisations, wages and salaries comprise the biggest single item of expenditure. Sometimes this expenditure is in the form of cash payments. This makes wages and salaries a tempting area for fraud and dishonesty. Here are some suggestions to help prevent dishonesty in your business.

Employ the Right Staff

Careful selection of staff is the first defence against incompetence and dishonesty. Staff obviously need to be honest and numerate. They need to be able to handle detailed rules and calculations. New staff should receive training or, at least, be given time to read payroll manuals, which will help them do their job. Payroll staff should not disclose confidential information to people inside or outside the business.

Work should be assigned to staff so that each individual has a clearly defined role. This makes it possible to trace back any mistakes or irregularities to the individual responsible. All payroll decisions should be subject to audit and review by a supervisor who has enough practical experience to spot mistakes before they cause problems.

Where possible, all wages and salary deductions should be charged to an individual manager's budget. That manager should sign to indicate that the worker is entitled to the payment. He will need to check that the gross wage/overtime/bonus/holiday pay etc shown on the pay calculation is correct.

The wages supervisor should check that tax, NI, Save as You Earn (SAYE) deductions etc have been made correctly. It is not unusual to find that directors' national insurance calculations are calculated in the same way as other employees which is not normally correct.

Security Checklist

There are many opportunities for fraud and mistakes. Here are a few areas where employees may be tempted to defraud the system.

- Create a dummy employee. The wages administrator draws the wage for that employee.

- Continue to pay an employee who has left. The wages administrator collects the employee's wage.

- Pay non existent casual workers. This is a particularly tempting fraud when the pay is below the PAYE and NI thresholds.

- Pay overtime or bonus payments to individuals who have not earned them. Split the proceeds with the individual concerned.

- Give holiday pay to individuals in excess of that allowed in the Contract of Employment.

- Create a fictitious foreign employee or consultant. This is particularly attractive since payments are remitted abroad with no deductions of PAYE and NI. The UK tax authorities are unlikely to audit these wage payments.

- Arrange to make inflated payments to casual staff/subcontractors/associates who then give back part of the payment to the individual perpetrating the fraud.

- Pay expenses and benefits to individuals who are not entitled to receive them, possibly in return for 'favours'.

- Unscrupulous employ*ers* have been known to retain PAYE and NI payments instead of paying the tax to the Inland Revenue. This can create difficulties for employees attempting to claim benefits if the company subsequently becomes insolvent.

- Unscrupulous employers have been known to create dummy pension schemes. Employees' pension contributions are then misappropriated.

- Check for differences between the amounts calculated on the P11s and the amounts shown on the payslips. It would be possible to misappropriate part of an employee's wage if the employee either couldn't be bothered to check his deductions or wasn't given enough detail to do so.

- It would be possible for an individual to misappropriate the proceeds of a Payroll Giving scheme or Save As You Earn scheme.

- Although Electronic Fund Transfer is an inherently safe way of transferring money, a miscreant who had access to the code words could transfer money illegally. There should be a limit on the maximum amount that can be made via EFT on any individual's wage payment.

- No employee should be responsible for calculating wage payments and signing cheques. There must be an independent authorisation to make payments irrespective of how the payment is made.

- A range of wage payments should be checked periodically from start to finish. This systematic approach could highlight problems which might not be discovered by occasional random checks.

End of Year Procedures

At the end of every tax year, each business has to send the Inland Revenue a summary of its employment records. This information is contained on:

- Forms P14 End of Year Summary
- Forms P35 Employer's Annual Return
- Forms P11D Higher Paid Return of Expenses and Benefits
- Forms P9D Lower Paid Return of Expenses and Benefits.

Some notes on the use of these forms follow.

Form P14

The employer must complete a form P14 for every employee for whom a P11 deductions working sheet has been used during the year. The P14 is a summary of figures entered on each employee's P11. An example of a P14 is shown on page 80. Notice that all of the information required on a P14 can be obtained from the P11 with the exception of the employee's private address and occupational pension scheme. Only 'contracted out' employers will have a 'contracted out' scheme number (see Section 11 for an explanation of 'contracted out'). Guidance notes for completing the form are written on the P14 on page 80.

You have to complete P14 in *triplicate*; fortunately, the Inland Revenue uses carbon impregnated paper so there is no need to use your own carbon paper or make photocopies.

The top two copies of form P14 are submitted to the Inland Revenue together with form P35 (which we will look at later). The Inland Revenue send the top copy to the DSS for their records and retain the second copy themselves.

Details to be Entered onto Form P14

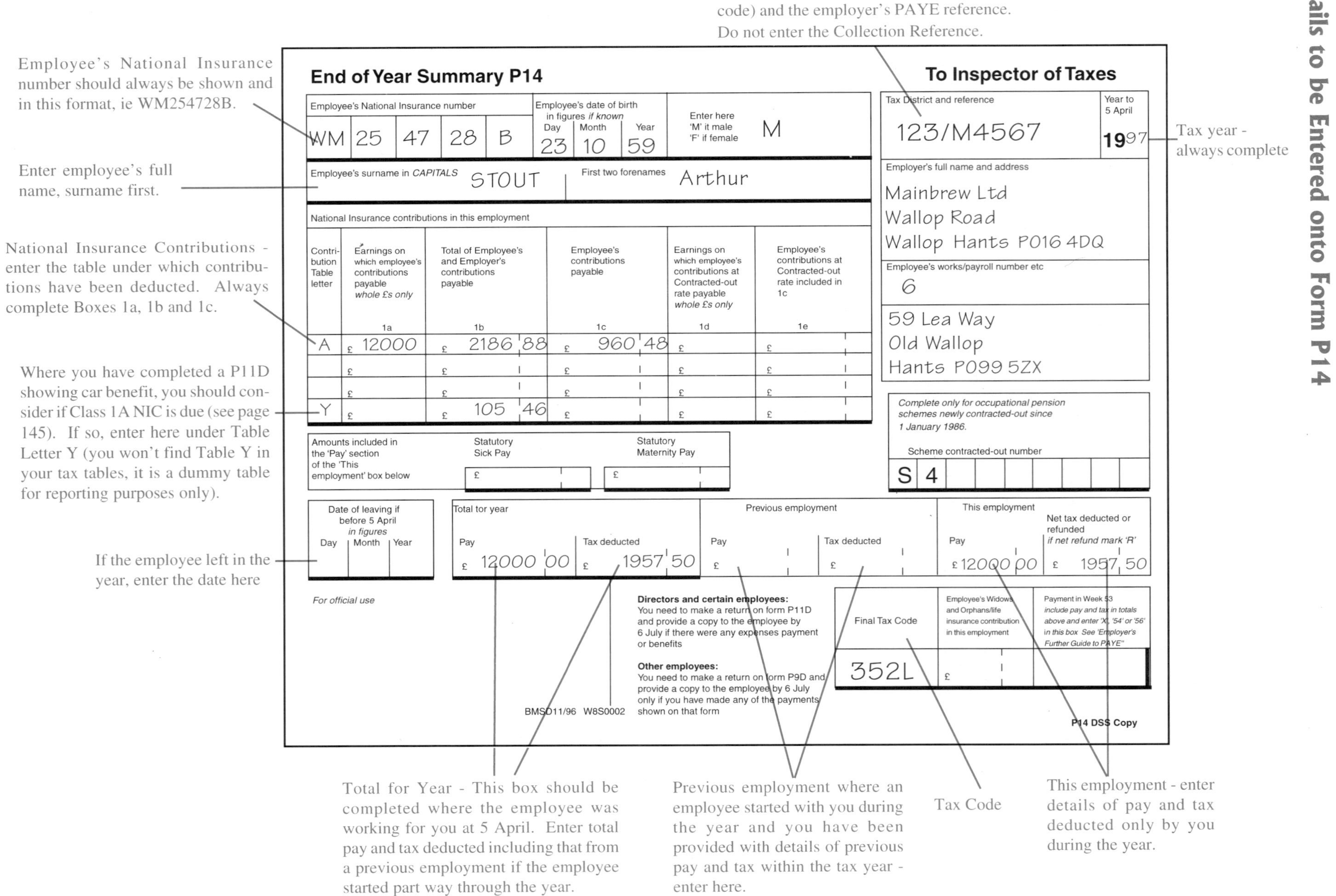

End of Year Summary P14 — **To Inspector of Taxes**

Employee's National Insurance number	Employee's date of birth in figures *if known* (Day / Month / Year)	Enter here 'M' if male 'F' if female
WM 25 47 28 B	23 / 10 / 59	M

Employee's surname in *CAPITALS*	First two forenames
STOUT	Arthur

National Insurance contributions in this employment

Contri-bution Table letter	Earnings on which employee's contributions payable *whole £s only* (1a)	Total of Employee's and Employer's contributions payable (1b)	Employee's contributions payable (1c)	Earnings on which employee's contributions at Contracted-out rate payable *whole £s only* (1d)	Employee's contributions at Contracted-out rate included in 1c (1e)
A	£ 12000	£ 2186.88	£ 960.48	£	£
	£	£	£	£	£
	£	£	£	£	£
Y	£	£ 105.46	£	£	£

Amounts included in the 'Pay' section of the 'This employment' box below	Statutory Sick Pay	Statutory Maternity Pay
	£	£

Tax District and reference	Year to 5 April
123/M4567	1997

Employer's full name and address
Mainbrew Ltd
Wallop Road
Wallop Hants P016 4DQ

Employee's works/payroll number etc
6

59 Lea Way
Old Wallop
Hants P099 5ZX

Complete only for occupational pension schemes newly contracted-out since 1 January 1986.

Scheme contracted-out number
S 4

Date of leaving if before 5 April *in figures* (Day / Month / Year)	Total for year: Pay	Total for year: Tax deducted	Previous employment: Pay	Previous employment: Tax deducted	This employment: Pay	This employment: Net tax deducted or refunded *if net refund mark 'R'*
	£ 12000.00	£ 1957.50	£	£	£ 12000.00	£ 1957.50

For official use

Directors and certain employees:
You need to make a return on form P11D and provide a copy to the employee by 6 July if there were any expenses payment or benefits

Other employees:
You need to make a return on form P9D and provide a copy to the employee by 6 July only if you have made any of the payments shown on that form

Final Tax Code	Employee's Widows and Orphans/life insurance contribution in this employment	Payment in Week 53 *include pay and tax in totals above and enter 'X', '54' or '56' in this box See 'Employer's Further Guide to PAYE'*
352L	£	

BMSD11/96 W8S0002

P14 DSS Copy

Employee's National Insurance number should always be shown and in this format, ie WM254728B.
Enter employee's full name, surname first.
National Insurance Contributions - enter the table under which contributions have been deducted. Always complete Boxes 1a, 1b and 1c.
Where you have completed a P11D showing car benefit, you should consider if Class 1A NIC is due (see page 145). If so, enter here under Table Letter Y (you won't find Table Y in your tax tables, it is a dummy table for reporting purposes only).
If the employee left in the year, enter the date here
Tax District and Reference. You should show the Tax District number (a three digit code) and the employer's PAYE reference. Do not enter the Collection Reference.
Tax year - always complete
Total for Year - This box should be completed where the employee was working for you at 5 April. Enter total pay and tax deducted including that from a previous employment if the employee started part way through the year.
Previous employment where an employee started with you during the year and you have been provided with details of previous pay and tax within the tax year - enter here.
Tax Code
This employment - enter details of pay and tax deducted only by you during the year.

The bottom copy of the P14 is P60 'Certificate of Pay, Income Tax and National Insurance Contributions'. This is given to the employee as his record of total pay, tax and national insurance deductions in the tax year. It is important that the employee retains form P60. It could be required by the Inland Revenue as evidence of their earnings if, for example, a tax refund was due at the end of the year. If the employee loses form P60, he cannot get his employer to provide a duplicate. Instead the employer should instruct the employee to get in touch with the Tax Office. If you have a number of employees, separate the top two copies of form P14 and put them into two piles - one for the DSS and the other for the Inland Revenue. Both piles are submitted to the Inland Revenue together with form P35 (see below). The Inland Revenue will issue employers with new P14 forms at the beginning of each tax year.

Form P35

Form P35 is called the Employer's Annual Return. It is a summary of Income Tax and National Insurance Contributions deducted from employees' wages. It also summarises Statutory Sick Pay and Statutory Maternity Pay recovered by the business. Employers are required to give details of each employee for which a deductions working sheet P11 has been raised during the year. An example of a form P35 is shown on pages 83 and 84.

Form P35 is an important document because it is a formal declaration to the Inland Revenue of the types of payment made to employees. The front of form P35 contains a 'checklist' which asks the employer a series of questions about benefits, expenses and overseas earnings. Each of these questions must be answered by ticking the appropriate box.

The form includes a 'declaration and certificate' on which the employer declares that he has submitted:

- A form P14 for every employee for whom a P11was prepared

- A form P38A (see pages 87 and 88) for employees for whom tax and national insurance have not been deducted. This form is important if you employ temporary or casual staff. If you sign this form, you declare that you hold a P46 for each worker and you paid them less than the single person's tax allowance. It would be foolish to sign the form unless you complied with the conditions as you wouldn't have a leg to stand on if you received an Inland Revenue PAYE audit. It might be worth rereading the notes about form P46 on page 62 in Section 6.

Back of Form P35

Page 84 shows the reverse of form P35. The top part of the form asks you to list all employees' names for whom a P11 has been completed during the year. If you have more than 10 employees, you will need a P35 Continuation Sheet to record the extra names and details. The Inland Revenue will not accept this information unless it is on one of their own continuation sheets. Be sure to check that the totals supplied for each employee on form P35 cross checks with the details supplied on the P14 forms.

The lower half of the back of form P35 contains a fearsome looking calculation of income tax and national insurance contributions now due. Instruction Card 20 from the Employer's Quick Guide (CWG1) gives limited guidance on how to complete this form. The following additional notes may be useful:

- Follow each letter in sequence entering the appropriate figures in each box from the totals of the P11 Deductions Working Sheets.

- It may be best to photocopy the form first and fill in the photocopy in case you make a mistake.

- Have your payment booklet handy so you can work out the total tax and national insurance paid to the Revenue to see if your figures agree.

Do not withold submission of forms P35 and P14s if you are behind with your payments of tax and national insurance collected. To do so would attract an additional, and unnecessary, penalty.

If completion of form P35 reveals that there is an additional amount of tax or national insurance due to the Inland Revenue, this should not be sent to the Inspector. Instead it should be sent to the **Collector** of Taxes.

Any payments made after 19 April following the end of the tax year will attract an interest penalty on the late payment. Late submissions of form P14 and P35 also attract a penalty.

Form P35 Front

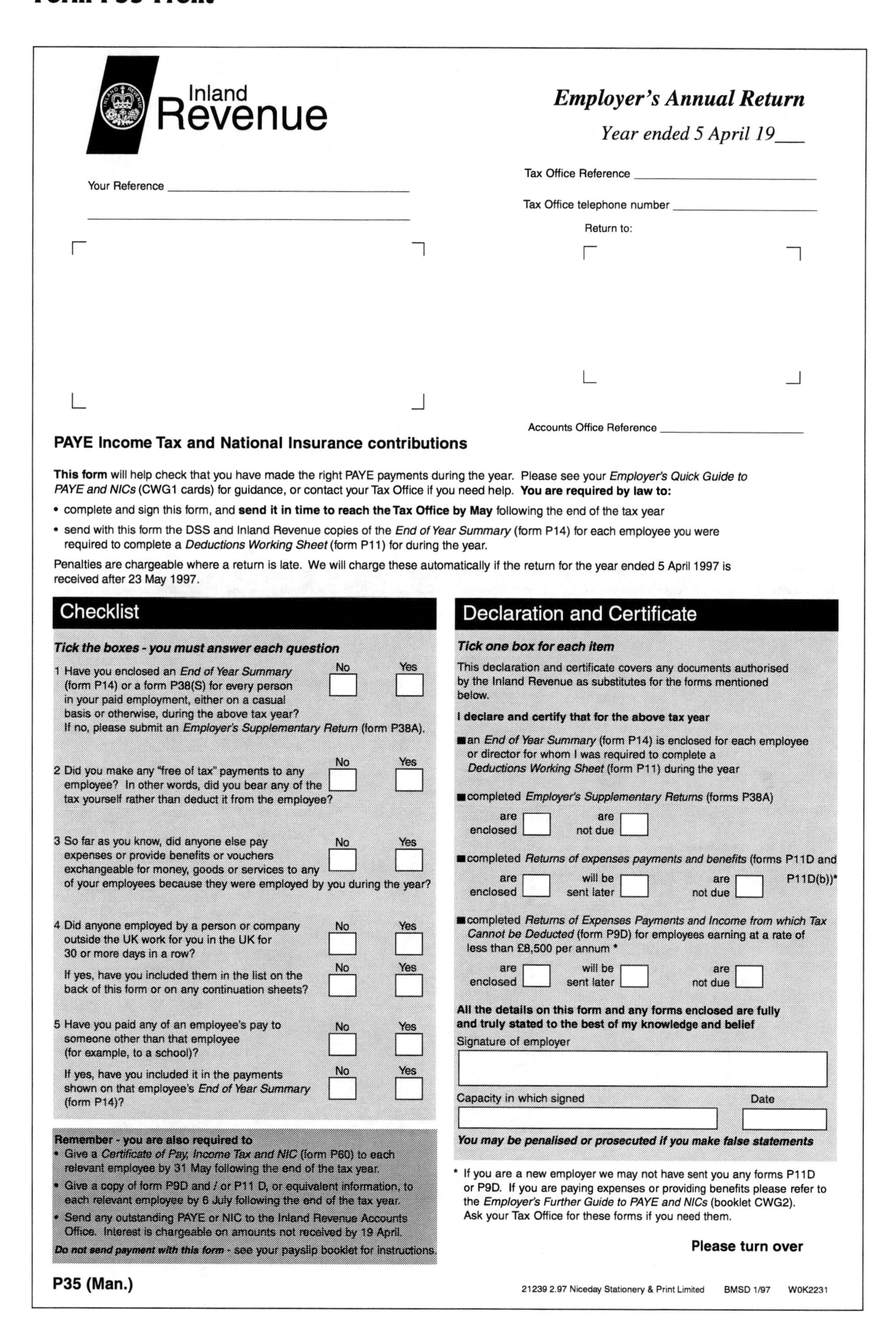

Inland Revenue

Employer's Annual Return

Year ended 5 April 19___

Your Reference ______________________

Tax Office Reference ______________________

Tax Office telephone number ______________________

Return to:

Accounts Office Reference ______________________

PAYE Income Tax and National Insurance contributions

This form will help check that you have made the right PAYE payments during the year. Please see your *Employer's Quick Guide to PAYE and NICs* (CWG1 cards) for guidance, or contact your Tax Office if you need help. **You are required by law to:**

- complete and sign this form, and **send it in time to reach the Tax Office by May** following the end of the tax year
- send with this form the DSS and Inland Revenue copies of the *End of Year Summary* (form P14) for each employee you were required to complete a *Deductions Working Sheet* (form P11) for during the year.

Penalties are chargeable where a return is late. We will charge these automatically if the return for the year ended 5 April 1997 is received after 23 May 1997.

Checklist

Tick the boxes - you must answer each question

1 Have you enclosed an *End of Year Summary* (form P14) or a form P38(S) for every person in your paid employment, either on a casual basis or otherwise, during the above tax year? No ☐ Yes ☐
If no, please submit an *Employer's Supplementary Return* (form P38A).

2 Did you make any "free of tax" payments to any employee? In other words, did you bear any of the tax yourself rather than deduct it from the employee? No ☐ Yes ☐

3 So far as you know, did anyone else pay expenses or provide benefits or vouchers exchangeable for money, goods or services to any of your employees because they were employed by you during the year? No ☐ Yes ☐

4 Did anyone employed by a person or company outside the UK work for you in the UK for 30 or more days in a row? No ☐ Yes ☐
If yes, have you included them in the list on the back of this form or on any continuation sheets? No ☐ Yes ☐

5 Have you paid any of an employee's pay to someone other than that employee (for example, to a school)? No ☐ Yes ☐
If yes, have you included it in the payments shown on that employee's *End of Year Summary* (form P14)? No ☐ Yes ☐

Remember - you are also required to

- Give a *Certificate of Pay, Income Tax and NIC* (form P60) to each relevant employee by 31 May following the end of the tax year.
- Give a copy of form P9D and / or P11 D, or equivalent information, to each relevant employee by 6 July following the end of the tax year.
- Send any outstanding PAYE or NIC to the Inland Revenue Accounts Office. Interest is chargeable on amounts not received by 19 April.

Do not send payment with this form - see your payslip booklet for instructions.

Declaration and Certificate

Tick one box for each item

This declaration and certificate covers any documents authorised by the Inland Revenue as substitutes for the forms mentioned below.

I declare and certify that for the above tax year

- an *End of Year Summary* (form P14) is enclosed for each employee or director for whom I was required to complete a *Deductions Working Sheet* (form P11) during the year
- completed *Employer's Supplementary Returns* (forms P38A)
  are enclosed ☐ are not due ☐
- completed *Returns of expenses payments and benefits* (forms P11D and P11D(b))*
  are enclosed ☐ will be sent later ☐ are not due ☐
- completed *Returns of Expenses Payments and Income from which Tax Cannot be Deducted* (form P9D) for employees earning at a rate of less than £8,500 per annum *
  are enclosed ☐ will be sent later ☐ are not due ☐

All the details on this form and any forms enclosed are fully and truly stated to the best of my knowledge and belief

Signature of employer

Capacity in which signed | Date

You may be penalised or prosecuted if you make false statements

* If you are a new employer we may not have sent you any forms P11D or P9D. If you are paying expenses or providing benefits please refer to the *Employer's Further Guide to PAYE and NICs* (booklet CWG2). Ask your Tax Office for these forms if you need them.

Please turn over

P35 (Man.)

21239 2.97 Niceday Stationery & Print Limited BMSD 1/97 W0K2231

Form P35 Back

Deductions Working Sheets

List here the individual *Deductions Working Sheets* (forms P11) which you have filled in during the year and which contain a figure under either of the headings shown.

If there is not enough space here to list all your employees please prepare continuation sheets.

Enter only the figures for 'this employment'

Employee's name Put an asterisk (*) beside the name if the person is a director	**National Insurance contributions (NIC)** Enter the total of the employee's and employer's NIC †	**Income tax deducted or refunded** Write 'R' beside amount to show a net refund
	£	£
	£	£
	£	£
	£	£
	£	£
	£	£
	£	£
	£	£
	£	£
	£	£
	£	£
	£	£
	£	£

† Include Class 1A contributions payable in the year, unless you paid these by the Alternative Payment Method.

Note: the columns for **SSP and SMP paid** have been discontinued, but the figures may still appear on some computer-printed continuation sheets. If so, please ignore them.

Calculation of NIC and Income Tax now due

National Insurance contributions (NIC)

Total from this page	A	£
Total from continuation sheets	B	£
Total NIC A + B	C	£
Received from Inland Revenue to pay SSP / SMP	D	£
C + D	E	£
Statutory Sick Pay **recovered**	F	£
Statutory MaternityPay **recovered**	G	£
NIC compensation on SMP see your payment record	H	£
NIC Holiday claimed	I	£
F + G + H + I	J	£
Total NIC payable to Accounts Office E - J	K	£
NIC already paid	L	£
NIC now due K - L	M	£

Remember to deduct amounts marked "R"

Income Tax

Total from this page	N	
Total from continuation sheets	O	
Total tax N + O	P	
Received from Inland Revenue to refund tax	Q	£
Tax deducted from sub-contractors see your *Contractor's Statement* (form SC35)	R	£
P + Q + R	S	£
Tax already paid	T	£
Tax now due S - T	U	£

Do not send Payment with this form. Send it to the Inland Revenue Accounts Office immediately. See notes overleaf.

Contracted-out pension schemes

Enter here your employer's contracting-out number, where applicable:

(You will find the number on the Occupational Pensions Board's Certificate)

§ I claim payment under Section 7 of the Social Security Act 1986 for each employee on whose *End of Year Summary* (form P14) I have entered a scheme contracting-out number. So far as I know, none of these employees is in an employment which has been contracted-out by reference to any other scheme since 1 January 1986. "✓"

§ You can only claim if this form is used for 1992-93 or earlier

Forms P11D and P9D

At the end of each tax year, an employer is obliged to send to the Inland Revenue a form P11D for any director and for any employee receiving expenses or benefits in kind who earns *more* than £8,500 a year including the value of benefits in kind.

Lower paid employees have a P9D

You must submit a form P9D for any employee receiving expenses or benefits in kind who earns *less* than £8500 per annum including the value of those benefits in kind. Details of how to complete forms P11D and P9D are given in Section 9 - Expenses and Benefits.

Form P35 together with relevant forms P14 (and P11D and P9D, if available at that time) should be submitted to the Inland Revenue by 19 May each year. Be sure to send the form off even if you still have tax and national insurance payments owing to the Inland Revenue. This is important because late submission of the form attracts the following automatic penalties.

Higher paid employees have a P11D

Penalties

Late submission attracts an automatic penalty and, possibly, interest payments. Here is a summary of the due dates and penalties for taxation payments, P14s, P35s, P11Ds and P9Ds.

Action	Date	Penalty/Interest
Date by which all PAYE tax and National Insurance contributions for 1996/97 should be made.	19.4.97	Interest accrues on all tax and NI paid after 19/4/97 to date of payment.
End of year documents P14 and P35 etc to be submitted to the Inland Revenue (legal requirement).	19.5.97	An automatic penalty will be imposed where a 1996/97 return arrives later than 2/6/97. The penalty is £100 a month for every 50 employees (or under) for each month or part month the returns are late. If returns remain outstanding for more than one year, a penalty of 100% of the tax and NIC due on 19/5/97 can be levied. Any incorrect return can result in a penalty of 100% of the tax and NIC underpaid.
Forms P11D and P9D for 1996/97 to be received by the Inland Revenue.	6.7.97	The late returns are subject to a penalty of £300 per form plus up to £60 per day per form if delay continues. An incorrect return is subject to a maximum penalty of £3000 per form.

Inland Revenue

To be filled in by the employer

Employer's name			
PAYE Tax Office		Tax District reference	
		Collection reference	

Employer's supplementary return - Workers for whom you have not completed a form P14 or a form P38(S) for the year 6 April 1997 to 5 April 1998

You must complete this form if you answered "No" to Question 1 on your Employer's Annual statement, declaration and certificate (form P35).

This form asks for details about payments made to people who worked for you during the year to 5 April 1998 but for whom you did not complete an end of year summary (form P14) or a form P38(S). You need to look at your records to answer the following questions **for each worker**.

1. Do you hold a form P46 completed at either Statement A or Statement B by the worker?
2. Was the worker paid less than £78.00 every week (or £338 if the worker was paid monthly)?
   (See note about pay aside)

If for each of your workers you are able to answer **YES** to both questions, **please sign the Declaration below and return the form. There is no need to to complete the back of this form.**

If the answer to either question is **NO** for any worker, please **complete the back of this form for any such worker.**

Declaration

I declare that for **each worker** for whom I have not completed an end of year summary (form P14) or a form P38(S),

- I hold a form P46 completed at either Statement A or Statement B by the worker
- he or she was paid less than £78.00 every week (or £338 if the worker was paid monthly)

Signature of employer ______________ Date ________

Note about pay

Remember that pay includes

- salaries
- wages
- fees
- overtime
- bonuses
- commissions
- pensions
- holiday pay
- payment in lieu of benefits in kind, for example board wages
- meal vouchers (if worth more than 15p a day)
- lump sum payments when employment ends (if more than £30,000)
- expenses payments or benefits for directors and employees earning at a rate of £8,500 a year or more
- vouchers which can be exchanged for cash, goods and services
- the cost of providing rent free accommodation
- transport vouchers
- amounts charged to employee's credit cards provided by you
- any other payment of emoluments to your employees
- any payment which the employee is liable to pay but that you pay for him or her.

This list does not cover all the items you should treat as pay. For more information see The Employer's Further Guide to PAYE and NICs, CWG2. If you are not sure about an item, ask your local Tax Office.

P38A(1997)

23606 1.97 Niceday Stationery & Print Limited BMSD1/97 W0H0075

P38A Back

If there is not enough space in either Section, please attach a separate sheet. When you have filled in all the details you need to give, please sign the Declaration below and return the form.

Section A
Enter in this section details for

- any worker who was paid more than £78.00 in any week (or £338 if the worker was paid monthly)

or

- any worker who was taken on for more than a week unless he or she was a harvest worker *(who should be entered in Section B - see below)*.

Full name of person employed *Please state Mr/Mrs/Miss/Ms* 1	Last known address 2	National Insurance number *if known* 3	Employed as *enter type of work done* 4	Dates employed If less than a full year From 5	To 6	Total pay for year ended 5 April 1998 (see notes overleaf) 7	For official use only 8

Section B
Enter in this section details for

- any worker who was paid more than £100 in total by you in the year ended 5 April 1998 who has not already been listed in Section A

and

- harvest workers. The Employer's Further Guide to PAYE and NICs, CWG2 tells you more about harvest workers.

Declaration
I declare that to the best of my knowledge and belief

- I have made no payments that need to be listed above, *or*
- that the details given above, and on the attached sheets, are correct and complete

Signature of employer ______________ Date __________

Self Assessment

Self assessment was introduced in the 1996/97 tax year. Self assessment requires employees to calculate their own tax liability based on information supplied by the employer. This information is supplied on the employee's P60. Employees receiving expenses and benefits in kind also need copies of forms P11D or P9D, as appropriate. In order to give employees sufficient time to complete their self assessment forms, the employer must meet strict deadlines. These deadlines are as follows.

Information Required by Employees

Key Information Required by Employees	Deadline Dates	Which Employers?
P60s detailing pay and tax. All employees require this information.	31 May 1997 for tax year 1996/97	All employers
Copies of P11D and P9D information for employees who receive expenses or benefits in kind (not covered by a dispensation). This includes ex employees who request this information.	6 July 1997 for tax year 1996/97	Employers who provide expenses or benefits (not covered by a dispensation)

Information Required by the Inland Revenue

Key Information Required by the Inland Revenue	Deadline Dates	Which Employers?
Send P14s and P35s	19 May each year	All employers
Date for P11D and P9D information to be sent to the Inland Revenue	6 July 1997	Employers who provide expenses or benefits (not covered by a dispensation)

Expenses and Benefits

Who is Affected by Expenses and Benefits in Kind?

The following pages introduce the tax rules on expenses and benefits in kind. Don't forget to consult the Inland Revenue's guidebook 'Expenses and Benefits, A Tax Guide' (Booklet 480). This will give more details than can be included here.

Tax is charged on benefits paid to:

- company directors
- those earning salary and benefits which together exceed £8,500 a year.

These are called 'higher paid employees'. Tax is levied on the value of the benefit. Generally, the value of the benefit is the cost to the employer of providing that benefit.

Surprisingly, the limit of £8,500 has not been altered since 1979 which means that each year more and more employees fall into the benefits trap.

Be careful if an employee leaves during the course of a year. If he/she was earning at a *rate* of over £8,500 per annum, including benefits, then the benefits are still taxable.

What is a Benefit in Kind?

A benefit in kind is any provision made by an employer over and above the employee's normal wage or salary. Typical benefits include a company car, petrol for private use, private medical benefits, low interest loans etc. All higher paid employees pay tax on the value of their benefits in kind. The Inland Revenue convert the benefit into a cash equivalent. The benefit then attracts additional taxes in the form of:

- higher income tax payments
- higher national insurance payments.

In this chapter, we will examine some of the more common benefits in kind including:

- Cars
- Fuel
- Company vans
- Mobile telephones
- Beneficial loans
- Accommodation
- Relocation expenses
- Private medical insurance premiums.

We will look at the income tax and national insurance implications.

Benefits on Company Cars

If an employer provides an employee with a company car which is available for private use then the employee has a taxable benefit. There is a further taxable benefit if the employer makes fuel available for private use. Under tax legislation, mileage between home and the workplace is deemed to be private mileage. Therefore, taking the car home at night constitutes private usage. Tax is assessed on both the car benefit and the fuel benefit.

Sally has a company car

Car Benefit

From 6 April 1994 car benefit has been calculated as 35% of the original manufacturer's list price of the vehicle plus the price of any optional accessories fitted to the vehicle. The list price of the vehicle refers to the manufacturer's published price, the day before the date of the car's first registration. The list price includes the vehicle, delivery charges and optional accessories. All prices include VAT and fitting charges. However, the price does not include vehicle excise duty (road tax). Accessories fitted *after* the car is made available to an employee will affect the benefit providing that the list price of the accessories exceeds £100 (including VAT, fitting charges and delivery). The value of the accessory must be added to the value of the vehicle. This will increase the amount of tax paid in the year of fitment and subsequent tax years.

If the employee makes a contribution towards the purchase cost of the vehicle then the taxable value of the car may be reduced accordingly. However, this is subject to a maximum reduction of £5,000. Where the employee pays for private use of the vehicle, the value of the taxable benefit is reduced pound for pound.

There is an upper limit of £80,000 on the list price of a vehicle including accessories for tax purposes. If the purchase price exceeds this figure, then the price for tax purposes will be deemed to be £80,000.

There are also special rules applying to 'classic' cars. A classic car is a vehicle over 15 years old at the end of the tax year. For tax purposes, the value of a classic car is the higher of:

- the original list price at registration, or
- the open market value, providing that the open market value exceeds £15,000.

The open market value of a classic car must include accessories. The open market value may be derived from the vehicle's insurance value or from general prices in the market. Once again, contributions from the employee towards the vehicle's purchase price can be taken into account up to the maximum of £5,000.

Classic cars have special rules

We have already said that car benefit is calculated at 35% of the manufacturer's list price including accessories. However, this benefit is reduced by 1/3rd if the employee covers more than 2,500 business miles a year. It is reduced by 2/3rds if the employee's business mileage exceeds 18,000 miles per year. This means that employees must keep a mileage log so that they can prove that they are entitled to the discount if challenged by the Inland Revenue.

If a car is only made available for part of a year to an employee, the limits for business mileage (ie over 2,500 miles and over 18,000 miles) are pro-rated to the periods when the car is actually available.

In addition to reliefs for exceeding 2,500 miles and 18,000 miles a year, employees can claim a further 1/3 discount if the car is at least four years old at the end of that tax year.

Let's look at a typical car benefit calculation.

Example

We will calculate the taxable benefit to Sally for private use of the company car for the 1997/98 tax year based on the following information. Sally was provided with a company vehicle on 6 April 1997 which had a 1500cc petrol engine. The car was first registered on 14 July 1992. The original list price of the car was £16,000 and accessories of £2,000 were fitted. Susan contributed £2,000 towards the purchase price of the vehicle. In the 1997/98 tax year, Sally travelled 19,000 business miles. She is required to make a contribution of £30 per month towards her private use of the vehicle. The calculation would be:

Car benefit is based on the original list price

	£
List price of vehicle	16000
Plus accessories	2000
	18000
Less: Contribution to purchase price	2000
Total Price	**16000**

Contd

Example (Contd)

	£
Basic benefit £16,000 x 35%	5600
Less: 2/3 for over 18,000 business miles	(3733)
	1867
Less: 1/3 for car over 4 years old at end of 1997/98	(622)
	1245
Less: Employee contribution 12 x £30	(360)
Taxable Benefit in kind	**885**

If Sally is a basic rate tax payer, ie 23%, she will have to pay
£885 x 0.23 = £203.55 in tax.

Fuel Benefit

An employee is taxed on the value of fuel bought by the employer which is used for private mileage; this includes travel between home and work. This is an additional taxable benefit over and above car benefit. Fuel charges are calculated by reference to fuel scale charges. These fuel scale charges are generally changed each year in the Autumn Budget Statement.

The charge depends on whether the vehicle uses petrol or diesel and the cubic capacity of the engine. Scale charges are applied regardless of the actual amount of private mileage. The car fuel scale charges applying from 6 April 1997 are given in 'Expenses and Benefits - A Tax Guide 480 (1997)' as:

Annual Scale Charge
1997/98

Petrol		Diesel	
	£		£
1,400cc or less	800		
1,401cc to 2,000cc	1010	2,000cc or less	740
2,001cc or more	1490	2,001cc or more	940

If the employee reimburses the employer for all private mileage then no taxable benefit in kind will apply for fuel. Given the level of the scale charges, it can be beneficial for an employee with a low private mileage to pay for his/her own private petrol. If an employee wants to do this, get him or her to keep a mileage log which details business mileage and private mileage.

On the other hand, if private mileage is at the level where the cost of the fuel outweighs the tax on the benefit in kind, then obviously it is more advantageous for the employee to accept the scale charge.

Example

If Sally received petrol for private use of the company vehicle, her combined benefit would be:

	£
Taxable benefit in kind car	885
Fuel benefit	1010
	1895

Providing Sally is a basic rate tax payer, she will now pay:

£1895 x 23% = £435.85 of tax.

Note 1: Tax is charged at the highest rate. If Sally were to become a higher rate tax payer, she would pay:

£1895 x 40% = £758.00 of tax.

Note 2: Her employer will also have to pay Class 1A national insurance on her benefit (this is covered in Section 12 - National Insurance).

Taxing Car and Fuel Benefits

Income Tax

The Inland Revenue collects car and fuel benefits by making an adjustment to the employee's tax code. You may remember that the employee's tax code is calculated by deducting the value of benefits in kind from the employee's personal allowances.

A Car Benefit?

Sometimes the value of the benefits in kind exceed the employee's personal allowances. When this happens, the Inland Revenue converts the excess benefit into a K code, see the example on page 69. The K Code is the means whereby benefits in kind are converted into taxable pay which is taxed throughout the year.

Class 1A National Insurance Contributions

Employers are required to pay a special class of National Insurance contribution (known as Class 1A contributions) on car and fuel benefits. This kind of National Insurance is only payable by employers. It is based on the combined car and fuel benefit charges for each employee. The rate of Class 1A contributions for 1997/98 is 10% of the combined car and fuel benefit. See page 141 for more information on Class 1A National Insurance contributions.

Value Added Tax

HM Customs and Excise levy VAT on fuel supplied by the employer for an employee's private use. In the past, many employees failed to keep records of fuel used privately. This made it difficult for HM Customs and Excise to calculate the amount of VAT to be charged to the employer. To avoid this problem, HM Customs and Excise apply a *standard* fuel scale charge which is deemed to cover the private mileage element. These scale charges are applied quarterly for each vehicle. They are dependent upon the cubic capacity of the vehicle and the type of fuel used.

Quarterly Fuel Scale Charges from 6 April 1997

Diesel Engine		**Scale Charge incl VAT** £	**VAT due per car** £	**Scale Charge (net of VAT)** £
Cylinder capacity	2000cc or less	185	27.55	157.45
	Over 2000cc	235	35.00	200.00
Petrol Engine		**Scale Charge incl VAT** £	**VAT due per car** £	**Scale Charge (net of VAT)** £
Cylinder capacity	1400cc or less	200	29.78	170.22
	1401cc - 2000cc	252	37.53	214.47
	Over 2000cc	372	55.40	316.60

The scale charges shown in the table above apply from 6 April 1997. However, they are applied to the next *complete* VAT accounting period beginning on or after 6 April 1997. This means that the VAT scale charge applies to the first clear quarter arising in the new tax year. There is no need to apportion scale charges between quarters.

Be aware that the scale charges are usually published inclusive of VAT so you need to extract VAT before filling in the VAT Return. We have extracted the 'VAT due per car' and shown the 'scale charge net of VAT' in the table shown overleaf.

'VAT due per car' is added to box 1 on the VAT Return. The 'scale charge net of VAT' is added to box 6 of the VAT Return (as shown below). Of course, your business may have many cars so you will need to add the totals to box 1 and box 6.

The VAT is the employer's liability and not that of the employee.

Completing the VAT Return

Box 1

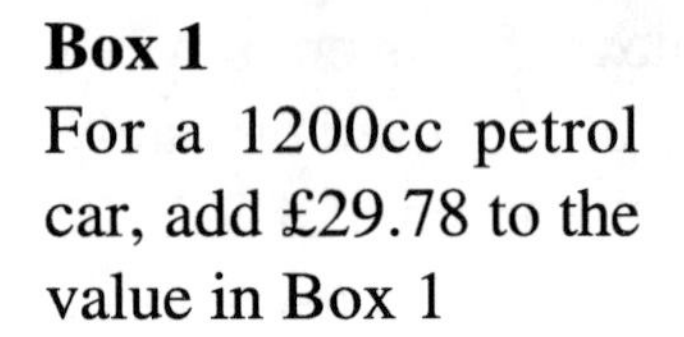

For a 1200cc petrol car, add £29.78 to the value in Box 1

Box 6

For a 1200cc petrol car, add £200 minus £29.78 to Box 6, ie add £170 (rounded to nearest pound).

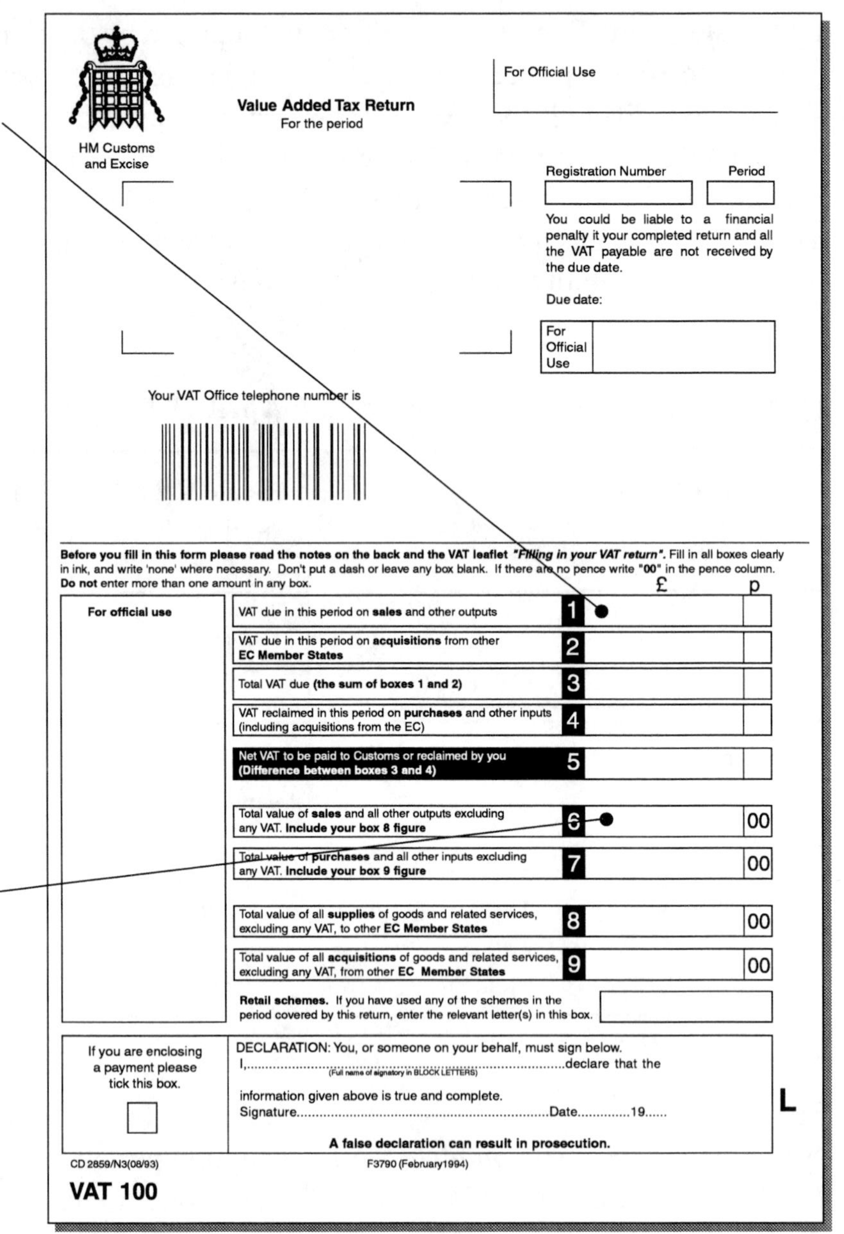

HM Customs and Excise

Value Added Tax Return
For the period

For Official Use

Registration Number | Period

You could be liable to a financial penalty if your completed return and all the VAT payable are not received by the due date.

Due date:

For Official Use

Your VAT Office telephone number is

Before you fill in this form please read the notes on the back and the VAT leaflet *"Filling in your VAT return"*. Fill in all boxes clearly in ink, and write 'none' where necessary. Don't put a dash or leave any box blank. If there are no pence write "00" in the pence column. **Do not** enter more than one amount in any box.

For official use		Box	£	p
	VAT due in this period on **sales** and other outputs	1		
	VAT due in this period on **acquisitions** from other **EC Member States**	2		
	Total VAT due **(the sum of boxes 1 and 2)**	3		
	VAT reclaimed in this period on **purchases** and other inputs (including acquisitions from the EC)	4		
	Net VAT to be paid to Customs or reclaimed by you (Difference between boxes 3 and 4)	5		
	Total value of **sales** and all other outputs excluding any VAT. **Include your box 8 figure**	6		00
	Total value of **purchases** and all other inputs excluding any VAT. **Include your box 9 figure**	7		00
	Total value of all **supplies** of goods and related services, excluding any VAT, to other **EC Member States**	8		00
	Total value of all **acquisitions** of goods and related services, excluding any VAT, from other **EC Member States**	9		00
	Retail schemes. If you have used any of the schemes in the period covered by this return, enter the relevant letter(s) in this box.			

If you are enclosing a payment please tick this box.

DECLARATION: You, or someone on your behalf, must sign below.
I,..declare that the
(Full name of signatory in BLOCK LETTERS)
information given above is true and complete.
Signature...Date.............19......
A false declaration can result in prosecution.

L

CD 2859/N3(08/93)   F3790 (February1994)

VAT 100

Providing Information to the Inland Revenue

From 5 April 1994, employers were obliged to notify the Inland Revenue quarterly of any employees becoming entitled to a company car. Employers are also required to report vehicle changes for existing company car holders. The quarters for reporting this information to the Inland Revenue are set at 5 July, 5 October, 5 January and 5 April.

Details of company car changes are notified to the Inland Revenue on a form P46(Car). An example of a form P46(Car) is shown on page 101. As you can see, the form shows:

- When the employee was first provided with a car, or
- When the employee was provided with a change of car, or
- When the employee was provided with an additional car, or
- When an employee already provided with a car started to earn at a rate of over £8,500 or became a director of the company, or
- When an employee is no longer provided with a car
- Whether fuel is provided for the employee.

The Form P46(Car) will also request details of:

- The make, model, engine size of the vehicle and whether it is petrol or diesel
- The original manufacturer's list price of the car and any additional accessories
- Any capital contribution paid to the cost of the car by the employee
- The expected annual business mileage of the employee.

This, of course, enables the Inland Revenue to keep an eye on part of your benefits position. We recommend that you set up records along the following lines for each employee who has a company car.

Employee Company Car Record

NAME:	National Insurance No: ...../...../...../...../.....

TYPE OF CAR PROVIDED:

Make and Model...

Engine Size/cc... Petrol or diesel.....................................

Date of Registration....................................	Manufacturer's list price of car (inclVAT, car tax and delivery charge) £....................................
Price of options and accessories (additional to standard equipment), incl tax, delivery and fitting, when car first made available to employee. £....................................	Price of accessories after car first made available (and after 31 July 1993) which had a price of more than £100. £....................................
Capital contributions made by the employee towards cost of car or accessories: £....................................	Annual payments for private use of car, where there is a requirement to make such payments: £....................................

Annual business mileage:

Less than 2,500 miles ☐ Between 2,500 and 17,999 miles ☐ 18,000 or more miles ☐

Date P46 (Car) sent to Inland Revenue: ....19.......

P46(Car)

Notification of a car provided for the private use of an employee or a director

Employer's name ____________________ PAYE reference ____________________

Employee's/Director's name ____________________ NI number [| | | |]

Part 1

You are required to make a return on this form for an employee earning at the rate of £8,500 a year or more or a director for whom a car is made available for private use. The completed form is required within 28 days of the end of the quarter to 5 July, 5 October, 5 January or 5 April in which any of the following takes place.

Tick whichever applies

1. The employee/director is first provided with a car which is available for private use ☐
2. A car provided to the employee/director is replaced by another car which is available for private use ☐
3. The employee/director is provided with a second or further car which is available for private use ☐
4. The employee starts to earn at the rate of £8,500 a year or more or becomes a director ☐
5. A car provided to the employee/director is withdrawn without replacement ☐

Part 2 Details of car provided

Make ____________________ Model ____________________ Date first registered ____________

Price of car (normally the list price at date of first registration) £ ____________

Price of accessories not included in the price of car £ ____________

Date of car first made available to employee ____________

Capital contribution (if any) made by employee to cost of the car and for accessories £ ____________

Sum payable (if any) by employee for private use of the car £ ____________ a week / a month / a quarter / a year

Is fuel for private use provided with this car? *yes* ☐ *no* ☐ If so, is the employee required to make good the cost of all fuel used for private motoring **and** do you expect him/her to continue to do so? *yes* ☐ *no* ☐

If the answer to the previous question is *'no'* please indicate the type of fuel *petrol* ☐ *diesel* ☐
and the cylinder capacity *up to 1400cc* ☐ *1401 - 2000cc* ☐ *2001 or more* ☐

If you have ticked box 1, 2, 3 or 4 in Part 1 please show the expected level of annual business mileage for this car *less than 2500* ☐ *2500 - 17999* ☐ *18000 or more* ☐

If you have ticked box 2 in Part 1 but the employee has more than one car available for private use please provide details or the car replaced

If you have ticked box 5 in Part 1 please provide details of the car withdrawn

} Make ____________________
Model ____________________
Date withdrawn ____________
(where appropriate)

Declaration

I declare that all particulars required are fully and truly stated according to the best of my knowledge and belief

Signature ____________________

Capacity in which signed ____________________

Date ____________________

P46(Car)

22977 9.96 Niceday Stationery & Print Limited CCO8/96 W0L2643

Company Vans

Sometimes an employer provides a van which is available to an employee for private use. In this case, the Inland Revenue will apply a flat rate benefit in kind charge on the employee. For this purpose, a van is defined as a vehicle built primarily to carry goods or other loads not exceeding 3,500 kilograms. Private use consists of anything other than business travel. It includes travel between home and the normal place of work. If the van is less than four years old at the end of the tax year then the flat rate benefit to the employee is £500. If the van is more than four years old, the benefit is £350.

The benefit can be reduced to take account of periods when the van was unavailable to the employee or is incapable of being used for 30 or more consecutive days. Where one or more vans are shared among several employees then the charge is shared between the various employees. There is, however, an overriding proviso that no employee can be charged more than the standard flat rate benefit. Any contribution by the employee towards private use of the van can be used to reduce the benefit in kind pound for pound.

Private use of a company van is taxable

Pooled Cars or Vans

Pooled cars or vans are not considered to be available for private use. This means that no taxable benefit arises providing that:

- the car or van can be used by any employee, ie it is not ordinarily used by one specific employee to the exclusion of others, and

- any private use of the vehicle is merely incidental to its business use, and

- it is not normally kept on or near the home of any of the employees overnight unless it is kept on the premises occupied by the provider of the vehicle.

Limited private use is allowed. For example, an employee could take a pool car home at night so that he/she can make an early start in the morning. Although the trip from office to home should really be considered 'private', this would not prejudice the claim for a pooled vehicle providing this is small compared to the length of the business trip. The Inland Revenue may challenge this relaxation of the rules if cases occur too often.

Employees Using their Own Vehicles

Sometimes employees use their own vehicles for business purposes. Often the employer pays a mileage allowance for the use of the car, or contributes to the running costs in some other way. Any contribution received by the employee is taxable.

Employees can use their own vehicles

The employer is obliged to record *all* contributions to employees' motoring costs on the employee's P11D. The employee must then make a separate claim annually to the Inland Revenue (on his self assessment form) to exclude the business element of his motoring expenses from being taxed. This claim offsets the taxable benefit shown on the P11D in part or in whole.

Reporting taxable benefit on the P11D and subsequently recovering the tax generates a lot of administrative work. This can be avoided by using the Fixed Profit Car Scheme (see below).

Employees' vehicle expenses are apportioned between business use and private use on a mileage basis. This means that employees should keep a mileage log to record business miles covered. The employee may claim for all the normal running costs of the car. They can even claim capital allowances to reflect depreciation on the vehicle in proportion to its business use. Usually the claim for tax relief neutralises the tax liability.

Fixed Profit Car Scheme

It is possible for an employer to adopt a special arrangement with the Inland Revenue whereby the employee is reimbursed the vehicle running expenses without there being any liability to tax. This can be achieved by either:

- a specific agreement with the Inland Revenue (called a dispensation), or
- more commonly, by using the Inland Revenue's fixed profit car scheme (FPCS).

The fixed profit car scheme enables an employer to make payments to an employee which are free of tax. This freedom from tax applies even if the employee is a director or earns over £8,500 per annum. Nor is there any need to include fixed profit car scheme expenses on the employee's P11D.

Mileage payments must be made in line with rates published annually by the Inland Revenue. The rates vary according to the engine size of the car. Details of the Fixed Profit Car Scheme are given in leaflet FPCS2(1997) 'Fixed Profit Car Scheme' working sheet' (see page 105). Some employers apply a flat rate reimbursement regardless of the engine size. Providing such payments are within the Inland Revenue's guidelines, they are deemed to be tax free. The rates for the fixed profit car scheme for the 1997/98 tax year are as follows.

Fixed Profit Car Scheme Rates per Mile 1997/98

Engine Size	First 4000 Miles in the tax year	Over 4000 Miles in the tax year
0 - 1000cc	28p	17p
1001 - 1500cc	35p	20p
1501 - 2000cc	45p	25p
Over 2000cc	63p	36p

If the mileage rate paid to an employee exceeds the rates specified in the fixed profit car scheme, the excess becomes taxable on the employee. The excess has to be included in gross pay and taxed. This excess will also be subject to Class 1 National Insurance contributions for both the employee (up to the employee's upper earnings limit) and employer.

Example

An employee travels 1,000 miles in a 1000cc motor car. He is paid 35p per mile by his employer. Tax would be calculated as follows:

1000 miles @ 35p	=	£35
1000 miles @ 28p (FPCS rate)	=	£28
Excess	=	£7

£7 would be added to salary and charged to both PAYE and NIC.

Employers have to obtain Inland Revenue approval before using the fixed profit car scheme. Before approval, the Inland Revenue will ask to see a sample of the claim forms submitted by employees for car usage.

There is no statutory requirement for an employee to be bound by the rules of the fixed profit car scheme. If the employee does not wish to use the scheme, he may submit a claim to his employer based on the actual running costs of the car adjusted for the proportion of business to private mileage (as discussed under 'Employees using their own vehicles' on page 103).

Form FPCS2

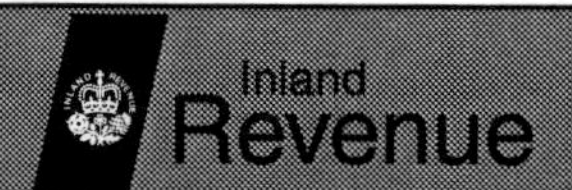

Fixed Profit Car Scheme
Information for Employee's Tax Return

Note for the employer

You do not have to use this form but if you have agreed a Fixed Profit Car Scheme with your Tax Office, you may find it a useful way of giving employees the information they need to complete their personal Tax Returns. You do not have to complete section 'A' if section 'B' is completed.

If you have agreed a Fixed Profit Car Scheme with your Tax Office do not put any of this information on form P11D or P9D. If a Fixed Profit Car Scheme has not been agreed with your Tax Office, car and mileage allowances must be entered on form P11D or P9D.

This form can be used for the year ended 5 April 1997 and later years. Forms are available from the Annual Pack Orderline (Phone 0345 646 646). You may find it helpful to keep a copy of each completed form as they could help you when dealing with any enquiries.

The term employee is used to cover both directors and employees throughout the rest of this form.

Employer's details

Employer's name | PAYE tax reference | Tax year

Employee's details

Employee's name | Works number or department | Tick here if a director | National Insurance number

Note for employee

A Fixed Profit Car Scheme is an arrangement which may agreed between the employer and the Tax Office to establish any profit element in motor mileage allowances. It reduces record keeping for employers and employees. The taxable profit is the excess of the mileage allowances over the 'tax free' amount set by the Inland Revenue.

Please keep this form in a safe place as you may not be able to get a duplicate. You will need it for your personal records and to complete your Tax Return if you get one. Box 1.15 on this form corresponds to the one that should be completed on your Tax Return. Your employer may not have completed Box 1.15 to show any taxable profit. If you

- need to work out the taxable profit from the other information provided
- require details of the 'tax free' mileage rates
- want further information

Leaflet IR125: Using your own car for work, is available from any Tax Office or Enquiry Centre.
The Tax Office may need to adjust your tax code to take account of the information on this form.

A. Car and mileage allowances paid for a car owned or hired by the employee

Give details of the total amount paid to the employee and the number of business miles for which payments were made in the year.

Only include car and mileage allowances within a Fixed Profit Car Scheme. If the employee has opted out of the agreement between the employer and the Tax Office, the allowances paid should be included on the form P11D or P9D.

	Gross Amount	Business miles for which payments made in year
Car or mileage allowance paid for employee's car	£	£

B Fixed Profit Car Scheme Profit

Employers are asked to complete box 1.15 below to show the Fixed Profit Car Scheme profit from the profit tables

	Taxable Profit
Fixed Profit Car Scheme profit from the tables	1.15 £

FPCS 2(1997)

23392 12.96 Niceday Stationery & Print Limited BMSD11/96 W0M0108

Mobile Telephones

Some employers provide their employees with a mobile telephone. If the employee earns more than £8,500 (including the value of benefits in kind) then the employee is liable to pay tax on that benefit. The benefit is currently valued at £200 per annum so that the cost to a standard rated tax payer would be £200 x 23% = £46 per annum. This reduces the employee's personal allowance so that the benefit is recovered in the employee's weekly or monthly 'pay packet'. The flat rate benefit charge can be avoided where there is no personal use of the mobile phone or, if there is personal use, the full cost of that use is refunded to the employer. This reimbursement does not need to include a proportion of the rental charge for the phone. The taxable benefit is not restricted to mobile telephones, it also applies to car telephones fitted into vehicles.

Beneficial Loans

It is quite common for an employer to provide an employee with a loan at either no interest or a more favourable rate than is generally available. Normally, the employee is liable to income tax on the interest saved as a result of the loan.

The value of the benefit is calculated by reference to an 'official' rate of interest. The official rate of interest is set by the Inland Revenue. The rate is influenced by bank base rates and current mortgage interest rates. These official interest rates are published in Expenses and Benefits - A Tax Guide 480 (1997) updated annually on form P11D(Int) available from the Annual Pack Orderline 0345-646-646 or your local tax office.

There are two methods used by the Inland Revenue to calculate interest on beneficial loans.

The first method is known as the 'average method'. This method averages the loan over the tax year by reference to the opening and closing balances at the beginning and the end of the tax year. It then applies the average official rate of interest over the period. An example of the averaging method is shown on page 108. The interest actually paid by the employee is deducted from the 'average' amount computed. The difference is chargeable to tax.

The second method, known as the 'alternative method', computes interest on the balance outstanding on the loan on a day-to-day basis by applying the official rate of interest to this balance. Once again, any interest paid by the employee is deducted from the amount calculated by the Inland Revenue.

The Inland Revenue adopts the average method unless the employee elects for the alternative method to be used.

Not all beneficial loans attract a tax liability. The Inland Revenue will allow the following exceptions.

- The employee earns less than £8,500 per annum including the value of the benefit in kind.
- The loan provided by the employer to the employee does not exceed £5,000 in any tax year.
- The loan is used to pay Inheritance Tax or Capital Gains Tax.
- The loan is used to buy a life annuity for someone aged 65 or over.
- The loan is advanced against expenses and does not exceed £1,000. The loan must be spent within six months, and the employee must account for the expenditure.
- The loan is used to buy plant or machinery for use in a partnership.
- The loan is made on the same terms as loans made by the employer to the general public.
- The loan is to acquire an interest in a close company or partnership or to improve commercially let property.

Let's look at an example using the average calculation method.

Example

Mainbrew makes a loan of £9,000 to Malcolm the Managing Director on 1 October 1997. The loan is repayable in three equal instalments of £3,000. Malcolm paid £100 interest between 1 October 1997 and 5 April 1998. The Inland Revenue's official rate of interest over the whole period of the loan was 7.5%.

- The first repayment of £3,000 was made on 1 January 1998
- The second payment of £3,000 was made on 1 April 1998
- The third payment of £3,000 is due on 1 July 1998.

Let's work out the taxable benefit on the loan for the 1997/98 tax year.

		£
1.10.97	Loan granted	9000
5. 4.98	Balance of loan outstanding (9000 - 6000)	3000
Average loan outstanding	$\frac{9000 + 3000}{2}$	6000
Period of loan =		274 days
Days in tax year 1.10.97 - 5.4.98 =		187 days
Interest at 6000 x 7.5% x 187/274		307
Deduct Interest paid in tax year		100
Assessable Benefit 1997/98 to be recorded by the employer on the employee's P11D		207

Loan Written off

Where an employer writes off a loan or a proportion of a loan to an employee, the amount that is written off will be treated as a cash payment in the year in which it is written off and subject to Income Tax. It will also be subject to National Insurance contributions as the amount written off is deemed to be earnings. The payment of tax and national insurance contributions on the written off portion applies in all circumstances. This applies even if the loan would not have incurred a tax liability as a beneficial loan.

Multiple Loans

If an employer grants more than one loan to an employee, the loans will be aggregated for the purpose of computing any benefit in kind.

Loans for House Purchase

Sometimes an employer provides an employee with a loan to buy a house. Providing the loan is used for that purpose, the first £30,000 of the loan will qualify for tax relief. However, during the current tax year (1997/98) the loan would only qualify for tax relief at the rate of 10% of any interest paid on the first £30,000.

Accommodation

In general, an employee is liable to pay tax on any living accommodation provided free by the employer. The value of the benefits depends upon several factors, these are:

- The rateable value of the property or the rent paid by the employer if higher.

- The running costs of the property such as lighting and heating. This applies to employees earning over £8,500 per annum.

- There is an additional charge where the cost of the property exceeds £75,000 or was worth more than £75,000 when the employee first occupied the property. The excess over £75,000 is multiplied by the official rate of interest at the beginning of the appropriate year of assessment.

There are, however, exceptions. Tax is not charged on accommodation if:

- Occupying the property puts the employee in a position to perform his duties properly, eg the provision of accommodation to a hospital doctor.

- The employment involves a specific security risk and special accommodation is provided by the employer to ensure the employee's safety.

- It is customary for that type of employment to have accommodation provided and where provision of such accommodation helps the employee to perform their duties, eg provision of on-site accommodation to school caretakers.

Relocation Expenses

Sometimes an employer pays an employee's relocation and removal expenses. Such expenses are tax free up to the current limit of £8,000. However, it is a condition that the employee has to move because of the nature of his employment. If an amount is paid in excess of £8,000 then the employee has to pay tax on the surplus. Typical expenses paid for by employers would include removal fees, estate agents' fees, survey fees, travel and subsistence payments in connection with the move, replacement of household items not compatible with the new home (eg carpets) and bridging loan interest. These expenses must be incurred and paid for by the end of the tax year following that in which the relocation occurs.

Private Medical Premiums

Some employers pay for their employees' private medical insurance. If the employee earns over £8,500 (including benefits), he will be taxed on the value of the medical insurance premiums. The benefit is recorded on the employee's P11D.

Other Benefits

Sometimes an employee is allowed to use assets like a company motor bike, television set, yacht etc. This use is taxed as a benefit. The benefit is assessed as its 'cash equivalent'. With the exception of land, the cash equivalent is the 'annual value' of providing that benefit. The 'annual value' is 20% of the market value of the asset at the time the asset was first provided. Where the employer charges some form of payment for use of the asset, this can be deducted.

Benefits Administration

At the end of each tax year, the employer must complete a Form P11D (Return of Expenses Payments and Benefits) for all directors and higher paid employees. An example of a Form P11D is shown on page 113.

The P11D requires the employer to supply a great deal of detail about employee benefits including:

- Assets transferred
- Payments made on behalf of the employee
- Voucher and credit cards
- Living accommodation
- Mileage allowance
- Car and car fuel
- Vans
- Interest free or low interest loans
- Mobile telephones
- Private medical care or insurance
- Relocation expenses
- Services supplied to the employee
- Assets placed at the employee's disposal
- Shares
- Subscriptions
- Expense payments.

To help you complete the return, a series of five working sheets are available for those who choose to use them. You do not need to submit the working sheets to the Inland Revenue. The five working sheets are:

- Working Sheet 1 - Living Accommodation (P11DWS1)
- Working Sheet 2 - Cars and Fuel Benefit (P11DWS2)
- Working Sheet 3 - Vans available for private use (P11DWS3)
- Working Sheet 4 - Interest Free and Low Interest Loans (P11DWS4)
- Working Sheet 5 - Relocation Expenses, Payment and Benefits (P11DWS5)

The figures arrived at from the working sheets are summarised on the form P11D. Once all P11Ds have been completed, the employer must make a declaration on form P11D(b) confirming that all forms P11D have been completed and sent onto the Tax Office.

These forms must be submitted to the Inland Revenue by 6 July each year. Late returns are subject to a penalty of £300 per form plus up to £60 per day per form for continued delay. An incorrect return is subject to a maximum penalty of £3,000 per form. As you can see, the penalties for non submission and incorrect forms P11D are very severe! One form P11D must be completed for each higher paid employee.

Employers must also complete a form P9D which is similar to form P11D (see page 115) for employees receiving benefits in kind earning less than £8,500 (including the value of benefits in kind). 'Lower paid' employees are not normally taxed on the value of benefits in kind received. However, the employer still has to submit a form declaring any benefits enjoyed by that individual. The statutory time limit for submission of form P9D is the same as that for the P11D.

The P11D should be completed in conjunction with the P11 Guide (1997) and Expenses and Benefits - A Tax Guide 480(1997). You will find that the following booklets give good background information on how P11Ds and self assessment fit together.

- SAT3 (1995) Self Assessment - What it will mean for employers, and supplement
- SA/BK1 Self Assessment - A General Guide.

P11Ds for People Still in your Employment

From April 1997 employers will have to complete the new style P11Ds. They will have to give one copy to the Inland Revenue and another copy to the employee. The employee's copy can be a photocopy of the form sent to the Inland Revenue. Alternatively, if you have a payroll programme or spreadsheet programme which produces a P11D substitute, the employee can be given that. Employees must receive their copies by 6 July. This is because employees who receive their tax returns need the information on the P11D to complete their self assessment returns. Employees who submit their self assessment returns by 30 September can pay tax due via an adjustment to their PAYE code for the following tax year. This avoids having to pay tax in a lump sum.

P11Ds for People who Leave your Employment

If an employee leaves you between the end of the tax year and 6 July following, post the P11D to the person's last known address.

If someone leaves your employment during the tax year, they have a right to request a copy of the P11D relating to the time they were employed by you. If they didn't request the information at the time of leaving, they have a right to be given the information on the P11D up to three years from the end of the relevant tax year.

Inland Revenue

P11D Return of expenses payments and benefits 1996-97

Note for employer
Complete this form for a director, or an employee who earned at a rate of £8,500 a year or more during the year 6 April 1996 to 5 April 1997. Do not include expenses and benefits covered by a dispensation or PAYE settlement agreement. Read the P11D (Guide) and booklet 480, [Chapter 24] before you complete the form. Send the completed P11D and form P11D(b) to the Tax Office. The forms must reach the Tax Office by 6 July 1997. You must give a copy of this information to the employee/director by the same date.
The term employee is used to cover both director and employees throughout the rest of this form.

Employer's details

Employer's name | PAYE tax reference

Employee's details

Employee's name | Works number or department | Tick here if a director | National Insurance number

Note for employee
Please keep this form in a safe place as you may not be able to get a duplicate. You will need it for your personal records and to complete your 1996-97 Tax Return if you get one. The box numbers on the form correspond to those on the employment pages of the Return. On this form P11D some boxes have the same numbering, for example 1.12. If there are entries in these boxes, you should add them all together and then include the total figure in the appropriate box on the Return, unless you think some other figure is appropriate. Your 1997-98 tax code may need to be adjusted to take account of the information given on this form.

A Assets transferred (cars, property, goods or other assets)

	Cost / Market value		Amount made good or from which tax deducted		Cash equivalent
Description of asset ______	£	-	£	=	1.12 £

B Payments made on behalf of the employee

Description of payment ______ 1.12 £

Tax on notional payments not borne by the employee within 30 days of receipt of each notional payment 1.12 £

C Vouchers and credit cards

	Gross Amount		Amount made good or from which tax deducted		Taxable Payment
Value of vouchers and payments using credit cards or tokens	£	-	£	=	1.13 £

D Living accommodation

Cash equivalent of accommodation provided for the employee or his/her family/household. 1.14 £

E Mileage allowance

	Gross Amount		Amount made good or from which tax deducted		Taxable Payment
Car and mileage allowances paid for the employee's car	£	-	£	=	1.15 £

F Cars and car fuel

If more than one car was made available to the employee, give details for each car and enter the total cash equivalent for all cars in box 1.16. If more than two cars were made available, either at the same time or in succession, please give details on a separate sheet

	Car 1			Car 2		
Make and model						
Date first registered						
Dates the car was available	From	To		From	To	
Business mileage used in calculation for this car If the car was unavailable for part of the year the business mileage limits are reduced proportionately ***Tick one box only for each car***	2,499 or less	2,500 to 17,999	18,000 or more	2,499 or less	2,500 to 17,999	18,000 or more
List price of the car *(if there is no list price or it is a classic car, employers see booklet 480; employees see leaflet IR 133)*	£			£		
Price of optional accessories fitted when the car was first made available to the employee	£			£		
Price of accessories added after the car was first made available to the employee	£			£		
Capital contributions (maximum of £5,000) the employee made towards the cost of the car or accessories	£			£		
Amount paid in the year by the employee for private use of the car	£			£		

Total car benefit charge for all cars available in 1996-97. 1.16 £

Total car fuel benefit charge for all cars available in 1996-97. 1.17 £

P11D(1997) BMSD 11/96

23386 12.96 Niceday Stationery & Print Limited BMSD11/96 WOP44

Please turn over

G Vans

Cash equivalent of all vans made available for private use.	1.18	£

H Interest free and low interest loans

If the total amount outstanding on all loans does not exceed £5,000 at any time in the year there is no need to complete this section.

	Loan 1	Loan 2
Purpose of loan(s) using code shown in P11D Guide		
Number of joint borrowers (if applicable)		
Tick the box if the loan is within MIRAS	☐	☐
Amount outstanding at 5 April 1996 or at date when loan was made if later	£	£
Amount outstanding at 5 April 1997 or at date when loan was discharged if earlier	£	£
Maximum amount outstanding at any time in the year	£	£
Total amount of interest paid by the borrower in the year to 5 April 1997 - enter "NIL" if none was paid	£	£
Date loan was made or discharged in the year to 5 April 1997 where applicable		
Cash equivalent of loan(s) - *after deducting interest paid*	1.19 £	1.19 £

I Mobile telephone

Cash equivalent of all mobile telephones provided.	1.20	£

J Private medical treatment or insurance

	Cost to you		Amount made good or from which tax deducted		Cash equivalent
Private medical or dental treatment or insurance	£	-	£	=	1.21 £

K Qualifying relocation expenses payments and benefits (Non qualifying expenses should be entered at P below)

Excess over £8,000 of all qualifying relocation expenses payments and benefits for each move. When calculating the excess you should take into account any qualifying items from last year.	1.22	£

L Services supplied

	Cost to you		Amount made good or from which tax deducted		Cash equivalent
Services supplied to the employee	£	-	£	=	1.22 £

M Assets placed at the employee's disposal

	Cost to you		Amount made good or from which tax deducted		Cash equivalent
Description of asset ______________	£	-	£	=	1.22 £

N Shares

Tick the box if during the year there have been share-related benefits for the employee ☐

O Other items

	Cost to you		Amount made good or from which tax deducted		Cash equivalent
Subscriptions and professional fees	£	-	£	=	1.22 £
Other items - please describe ______________	£	-	£	=	1.22 £

	Tax paid
Income tax paid but not deducted from the director's remuneration	1.22 £

P Expenses payments made to, or on behalf of, the employee

	Cost to you		Amount made good or from which tax deducted		Cash equivalent
Travelling and subsistence payments	£	-	£	=	1.23 £
Entertainment - *if you are a trading organisation, read P11D Guide and enter* ***either*** *"✓"* ***or*** *"x" as appropriate here* ☐	£	-	£	=	1.23 £
General expenses allowance for business travel	£	-	£	=	1.23 £
Payments for use of home telephone	£	-	£	=	1.23 £
Non-qualifying relocation expenses (those not in section K)	£	-	£	=	1.23 £
Other expenses - please describe ______________	£	-	£	=	1.23 £

P9D Return of expenses payments and income from which tax cannot be deducted 1996-97

Note for employer
Complete this form if you made expenses payments or provided benefits to an employee but have not completed a form P11D for the employee because he/she earned at a rate of less than £8,500 1996-97.
Brief notes are included on this form. Inland Revenue booklet 480 - "Expenses and Benefits - A tax guide" gives more detailed information. References to this booklet are given in the relevant sections.
Send the completed P9D to the Tax Office by 6 July 1997.
You must give a copy of this information to the employee by the same date.

Employer's details

Employer's name

PAYE tax reference

Employee's details

Employee's name

Works number or department

National Insurance number

Note for employee

Please keep this form in a safe place as you may not be able to get a duplicate. You will need it for your personal records and to complete your 1996-97 Tax Return if you get one. On this form some boxes have the same numbering, for example 1.12. If there are entries in these boxes, you should add them all together and then enter the total figure in the appropriate box on your personal Tax Return unless you think some other figure is appropriate.

A(1) Expenses payments

If the employee paid expenses solely and necessarily in the performance of his or her duties and you repaid the amount of those expenses, you do not need to include them here

Total all expenses payments including

- payments that included Value Added Tax (VAT), even if the VAT was later recovered from HM Customs and Excise
- round sum allowances
- all relocation expenses payments and benefits (see note below).

Some relocation expenses qualify for relief (see booklet 480 Chapter 5 and Appendix 7). The maximum amount that can be paid for any one move is £8,000. You should total all qualifying payments made for each move including

- any payments made in 1995-96, and
- any benefits provided under the relocation package in 1996-97 or 1995-96.

The **excess over £8,000** of any qualifying expenses payments and benefits for each move should be included in the total expenses payments figure entered below.

If the above amounts total £25 or less they do not need to be returned.

If more than £25 enter the total amount 1.23 £

A(2) Any other payments or benefits

Include here

- payments made to the employee and not included on the End of Year Return for 1996-97.
- payments made on the employee's behalf
- gifts in kind - enter the second hand value of any goods provided. That is, the price at which the employee could sell the items as soon as he or she got them.
- any other payments or benefits which could be turned into money not included elsewhere.

Employee's own National Insurance paid by you 1.23 £

Employee's personal telephone bills paid by you 1.23 £

Gifts in kind, for example Christmas hampers, presents etc 1.23 £

Anything bought for or paid to employee at other than market value 1.23 £

Any payment or benefit not included elsewhere *enter the value here and give details of the benefit in the box overleaf* 1.23 £

P9D (1997)

Please turn over

23385 12.96 Niceday Stationery & Print Limited BMSD11/96 WOP0043

B Vouchers and credit cards

Enter the expense of providing the vouchers and the goods and services for which they can be exchanged. Exclude the value of any vouchers, such as cash vouchers, which have suffered tax under PAYE.

Travel and transport vouchers, including season tickets | 1.13 £

Gift vouchers, including National Savings Certificates and Premium Bonds | 1.13 £

Meal vouchers that do not comply with the conditions in paragraph E5, Employer's Further Guide to PAYE | 1.13 £

Any other vouchers exchangeable for goods and services | 1.13 £

Credit cards provided for employees and their families - *enter the total amount of expenses met by credit card provided by you for the employee to use unless you have already entered these expenses under one of the above headings.* | 1.13 £

C Accommodation

Give the cash equivalent of accommodation provided for the employee and/or his of her family/household. Deduct any amounts paid by the employee towards the cost of providing the accommodation, for example, rent.

If the employee is provided with living accommodation give details of the rateable value. This is the gross value which applied before Community Charge was introduced. If the property did not have a gross value, enter "No rateable value established" and give your estimate of what the gross value would have been if rates had continued. If the property costs more than £75,000 special rules apply, see booklet 480 paragraphs 21.16 to 21.22.

If as well as providing the accommodation you paid some of the employees bills (such as heat and light) show these in the appropriate other box or boxes overleaf, whether or not the value of the accommodation itself is exempt from tax.

Enter property address

Enter rateable value of property £

Enter rent and insurance borne by you £

The cash value of accommodation provided is the greater of the above figures. Enter that figure here. | 1.14 £

Where necessary use this box to describe the benefits mentioned above and overleaf.

Return of Expenses and Benefits
Employer's Declaration

1996-97

As an employer you must complete a Return of Expenses payments and Benefits (form P11D) for each employee paid at a rate of £8,500 a year or more and for each director if

- *you have provided them with expenses or benefits which are not covered by a dispensation or PAYE settlement agreement*
- *you have arranged for expenses or benefits to be provided by a third party.*

Use this declaration to confirm that you have completed and returned the forms P11D for the year ended 5 April 1997.

Send this declaration with the completed forms P11D to reach your PAYE Tax Office by 6 July 1997. If you choose to send forms P11D in batches, send this form with the final batch.

By completing and returning this declaration you will satisfy the declaration and certificate on the Employer's Annual Return (form P35) that completed Returns of Expenses and Benefits (form P11D and/or form P11D(b)) are enclosed or will be sent later. For more information see the P11D Guide.

Employer's details

Please complete

Employer's name ______________________ PAYE tax reference ____________

Declaration

Tick the relevant box(es) and fill in the appropriate details.

☐ No expenses payments or benefits of the type to be returned on form P11D have been or will be provided for the year 1996-97. For this reason no forms P11D are attached.

☐ I confirm that all details of expenses payments and benefits that have to be returned on forms P11D for the year 1996-97 are enclosed with this declaration. I declare that the details on these forms are fully and truly stated to the best of my knowledge and belief.

☐ Forms P11D for the year 1996-97 were sent to ____________ Tax office on ____________
I confirm that all the details of expenses payments and benefits that have to be returned on forms P11D have been sent to the Tax Office. I declare that the details on these forms are fully and truly stated to the best of my knowledge and belief.

Signature of employer ______________________ **Date** ____________

Capacity in which signed ______________________

Please remember to give each employee/director a copy of their P11D information by 6 July 1997

P11D(b) (1997)

23384 12.96 Niceday Stationery & Print Limited BMSD11/96 WOJ0022

Section 10

Directors' Pay

In principle, directors are taxed according to the same PAYE rules as everyone else. In practice, some directors receive their remuneration in unusual ways. This can give rise to problems when assessing their pay and benefits for taxation purposes. Here are some points to watch out for.

Expenses and Benefits

In Section 9 we looked at a wide range of expenses and benefits which are taxable. These are detailed in:

- Expenses and Benefits - A Tax Guide - 480
- Chapter 5 of the Employer's Further Guide to PAYE and NICs CWG2 (1997)
- The P11D Guide.

Apart from a few, very special exceptions, all directors are taxed on their expenses and benefits. This applies *irrespective of whether they earn over* £8,500 per annum. All expenses and benefits must be reported on the director's P11D.

The term 'directors' has quite a wide meaning; it includes anyone who manages the affairs of a profit making body or society. It also includes anyone who instructs directors, such as a company chairman or president.

Salary Payment Dates

Many directors receive a monthly salary like everyone else in the business. However, sometimes a director's remuneration includes unusual or irregular payments like bonuses or awards. These additional payments are taxable; moreover, you have to be careful to tax them at the right time. The Inland Revenue guidance is contained on page 7 of the Employer's Further Guide to PAYE and NICs.

In general, pay should be taxed as soon as the director is *entitled* to receive payment. This applies even if the payment is not taken until a later date. For directors, the date when tax is payable is the earliest of:

- The date the payment is made
- The date the director is *entitled* to be paid
- The date the payment is *credited* to an account which the director can draw on, even if the director cannot draw on that account immediately
- The date when the remuneration is *decided.*

Occasionally, the business may decide to make a loan to a director as an advance on payment of salary or bonus. If this happens, the payroll administrator is required to account for PAYE on the advance as soon as the advance is made.

Payment dates are important for directors

Directors' National Insurance

We will look at National Insurance in detail in Section 12. However, this is a good time to mention that National Insurance Contributions for directors have special treatment. In fact, there is a whole DSS booklet devoted to directors called 'National Insurance for Company Directors', code CA44(NI35) from April 1995. The rules for directors' National Insurance Contributions (NICs) are complex.

Most problems stem from the way directors are paid. For example, a director could receive a modest salary throughout the year which is supplemented by periodic bonuses based on business performance. If deductions were based solely on the monthly earnings then the director's NICs would be low for most months of the year. However, during months when a bonus is paid, the director's NICs would be capped. This means that, on average, the Contributions Agency would collect smaller contributions from a director compared to an employee paid the same amount evenly over the course of a year.

To avoid this problem, directors' NICs are normally based on the *cumulative* earnings for the current tax year. Credit is then given for any NICs already made during the tax year. The balance of national insurance owed is then paid to the Collector of Taxes. An example will make the method clearer.

Calculating Directors' NICs

For the purposes of illustration, let's take a director who earns £2,500 per month in 1997/98. Here are the steps you need to take to work out his NICs.

First, set out the annual national insurance Class 1 earnings brackets. For 1997/98, these would be as follows:

Earnings Brackets (Annual) £	Employee's Contribution %	Employer's Contribution %
0 - 3,223.99	Nil	Nil
3,224.00 - 5,719.99	*2/10**	3
5,720.00 - 8,059.99	*2/10**	5
8,060.00 - 10,919.99	*2/10**	7
10,920.00 - 24,180.00	*2/10**	10
Over 24,180	Nil	10
* 2% payable on first £3224 pa	** 10% payable on earnings over £3224 pa	

Employees' Contributions

Have a look at the column labelled 'Employee's Contributions' in the table above. Directors who earn below £3,224 per annum do not pay national insurance. Once earnings reach £3,224 per annum, national insurance is paid on the *whole* of the earnings. However, the *first* £3,224 of earnings only attracts employees' national insurance contributions at the rate of 2%. Employees earning *over* £3,224 per annum attract national insurance at the rate of 10%.

Notice that there is a contributions ceiling for the employee. Earnings over £24,180 per annum do not attract additional NICs.

Employers' Contributions

Have a look at the column labelled 'Employer's Contributions' in the table above. Employers of directors who earn less than £3224 pay no employers' NICs. Once the director's earnings reach £3224 per annum, the employer has to pay NICs on the whole of the earnings. The level of contribution depends on the total remuneration for the year. NICs are levied at rates of 3%, 5%, 7% and 10% depending on the level of the earnings. Notice that there is no ceiling on employers' contributions. If directors earn over £24,180, NICs are levied at 10% of the earnings no matter how high those earnings may be.

The Monthly Calculation of Directors' NICs

Month 1

NICs are based on the total (ie cumulative) pay to date. In Month 1, the cumulative pay is £2,500. As the 'total pay to date' falls below the lower threshold (£3224), no NIC is paid either by the employer or employee. Here is the calculation.

	Cumulative Pay	Employee's NIC		Employer's NIC		Combined Employee/ Employer NICs Due
	£	%	£	%	£	£
Month 1	2500	Nil	Nil	Nil	Nil	Nil

Month 2

In the second month of the tax year, the director would receive a further £2,500 of salary bringing his cumulative pay to £5,000 for Month 2. The NIC position would be:

The employee's NIC is calculated as follows:

Pay		NICs Due
£3224 @ 2%	=	£64.48
£1776 @ 10%	=	177.60
£5000		£242.08

The employer's NIC is calculated as follows:

Pay		NICs Due
£5000 @ 3%	=	£150.00

	Cumulative Pay	Employee's NIC		Employer's NIC		Combined Employee/ Employer NICs Due
	£	%	£	%	£	£
Month 1	2500	Nil	Nil	Nil	Nil	Nil
Month 2	5000	2/10	242.08	3	150.00	392.08

Since no NICs have been paid to date, the total due at the end of Month 2 is £242.08 + £150.00 = £392.08.

Month 3

Total cumulative pay at the end of Month 3 will be £7,500. This gives the following cumulative pay position:

The employee's NIC is calculated as follows:

Pay		NICs Due	
£3224 @ 2%	=	£64.48	
£4276 @ 10%	=	427.60	
£7500		£492.08	
		242.08	Less paid Month 2
		£250.00	Payable Month 3

The employer's NIC is calculated as follows:

Pay		NICs Due	
£7500 @ 5%	=	£375.00	
		150.00	Less paid Month 2
		£225.00	Payable Month 3

	Cumulative Pay	Employee's NIC		Employer's NIC		Combined Employee/ Employer NICs Due
	£	%	£	%	£	£
Month 1	2500	Nil	Nil	Nil	Nil	Nil
Month 2	5000	2/10	242.08	3	150.00	392.08
Month 3	7500	2/10	250.00	5	225.00	475.00

Remaining Months of the Year

The calculation of employee's and employer's NICs continue for the remainder of the tax year along the lines shown above.

Once the employee's earnings reach £24,180, no further employ*ee*'s contributions are paid. However, the employ*er* must still continue to calculate NIC payments at the employer's top rate of 10%.

Directors who Receive Regular Remuneration

From 6 April 1997, any director who receives all of his remuneration on a regular monthly basis can opt to have national insurance contributions calculated on the same basis as other employees.

Pension Schemes

Everyone who has a satisfactory record of national insurance contributions is entitled to the *basic* state pension when they reach retirement age. However, most employees will want to supplement this basic pension by making additional contributions to a pension scheme. Employees have a choice of several ways of making these additional contributions. They can belong to:

- A pension scheme run by the government called SERPS. SERPS stands for State Earnings Related Pension Scheme.
- A pension scheme run by the employer. These schemes are called Approved Occupational Pension Schemes.
- A pension scheme run by an independent pension company. These schemes are called Personal Pension Schemes.

The purpose of this section is to provide background information on each type of scheme and point out specific payroll consequences which could affect the payroll administrator.

SERPS

SERPS is a pension scheme run by the government which enables employees to receive more than the basic state pension. In broad outline, it operates under similar rules to a commercial pension scheme. This means that the more you pay in, the more you expect to receive on retirement. Contributions into SERPS are made via National

Insurance Contributions. Employees who are contracted into the state scheme pay 'contracted in' NICs (see page 135 for 'contracted in' rates). Employees who are not contracted into the state scheme pay 'not contracted in' NICs (see page 136 for 'not contracted in' rates).

Notice that 'contracted in' contributions are higher than 'not contracted in' contributions. There is a simple explanation for this. Employees who are not contracted into SERPS make their additional pension contributions into a private pension scheme. Notice that there is a ceiling on the amount of national insurance that an employee is expected to contribute.

Payroll administration for employees contributing to SERPS is very simple. NIC deductions are made from gross pay using the 'not contracted out' tables CA38. More details of national insurance follow in the next section.

You do not have to belong to the state scheme. If you contract out of SERPS, you will normally make pension provision either through an employer's occupational pension scheme or through a personal pension scheme. Let's have a look at these schemes.

Employers' Occupational Pension Schemes

We have seen that employees are free to contract out of SERPS and join an employer's occupational pension scheme. This can be attractive because employers often contribute to their employees' pension scheme. This should lead to a higher pension for the employee at the end of the day. These schemes have various names; for example, they could be called:

- Company Pension Schemes
- Employers' Schemes
- Approved Occupational Pension Schemes.

Don't be confused by the different names, they all mean the same thing.

If your business decides to operate its own pension scheme, it will usually approach a pension provider to manage the scheme on the business' behalf. The pension provider will invest the pension payments to generate the best investment growth on behalf of the fund members.

Upon retirement, employees receive a pension based on their contributions plus any tax free growth which has accumulated in the fund. Employees are usually allowed to take part of their pension as a tax free lump sum but the balance must be used to buy an annuity. The annuity then provides their regular monthly pension payment.

Employers are free to vary the rules of the scheme as they see fit. Normally, both the employer and the employee contribute to the scheme. Most occupational pension schemes set a normal retirement age for the employee; however, this does not have to be the same as the state retirement age. The employer appoints trustees who deal with the pension provider and look after the interests of the fund members.

It is very important that the employer's pension scheme is approved by the Inland Revenue's Occupational Pensions Board. Approval brings important tax advantages for the employee. The Occupational Pensions Board has very strict rules concerning the conduct and administration of approved pension schemes. The Pensions Board issues a formal approval certificate when satisfied that the scheme is properly set up and run.

Payroll Implications for Employers' Schemes

If you hold an approval certificate from the Occupational Pensions Board and your pension scheme is contracted out of SERPS, you are entitled to deduct 'not contracted in' national insurance contributions for those employees covered by the pension scheme. However, in practice, many employers contine to deduct national insurance at the 'not contracted out' rate. At the end of the tax year, the DSS rebate the difference in contribution rates back into the employee's private pension scheme. Check what actions you should take with your pension scheme administrator. The DSS can handle the rebates easily because a certificate is provided by the pension provider for each employee who contracts out of SERPS. Remember, national insurance is always levied on the gross wage (ie before deduction of pension contributions).

Payments made into an approved occupational pension scheme are free of income tax. This means that you record the employee's pay *net* of pension contributions on the P11. Calculate income tax on the net (ie lower) figure. The net figure is also used on the end of year reporting forms (eg form P14 etc). In payroll jargon, this is called the 'net pay' arrangement.

We have said that contributions into an approved employer's pension scheme are free of tax. This is true. However, there is a ceiling on the amount of money that an employee can contribute in this way. At the time of writing these notes, this ceiling is 15% of the employee's gross salary in the tax year, including the value of benefits in kind.

By the way, employ*ers*' contributions to approved pension schemes are also free of tax. However, the tax applying here is, of course, Corporation Tax or Schedule D income tax, depending on the tax status of the employer.

Additional Voluntary Contributions (AVCs)

We have said that the *maximum* employee's tax free contribution to an approved pension scheme is 15% of the employee's wage in any tax year. However, it would be unusual for a scheme to set 15% as the *normal* contribution rate. Typically, employees are only required to contribute around 5% - 6% of their gross salary. If an employee fears that contributions at this level will not meet their needs in retirement, they can opt to make additional voluntary contributions (AVCs). An employee is allowed to make AVCs up to the maximum tax free allowance of 15% of gross wage.

AVCs are paid directly into the company's occupational pension scheme where they will grow alongside the other contributions and, ultimately, increase that employee's pension benefits.

Payroll Implications for AVCs

From a payroll point of view, AVCs are treated in exactly the same way as normal pension contributions. They are deducted from gross salary. It is not the job of the payroll administrator to check that the employee is within the maximum limit as this will be checked by the company pension advisor. AVCs are allowed up to the point where the projected pension equals two thirds of final salary.

Free Standing Additional Voluntary Contributions (FSAVCs)

We have said that employees who are members of an occupational pension scheme can make AVCs to their company scheme. However, employees are also free to make pension contributions to an alternative pension scheme if they want to. Contributions to these alternative pension schemes are called Free Standing Additional Voluntary Contributions (FSAVCs). Employees choosing to make FSAVCs to alternative schemes obviously hope that the performance of the alternative fund will be better than that of the company pension fund. FSAVCs are limited by the 'two thirds of final salary rule' just like AVCs.

Payroll Implications for FSAVCs

FSAVCs are treated differently to AVCs. Individuals make their FSAVCs contributions out of their taxed income. The payroll office does not provide for any tax relief. In practice, the employee will receive tax relief but this will be recovered by the pension fund directly from the Inland Revenue.

Here is an example. If a standard rated tax payer makes a payment of £77 into his pension using an FSAVCs contribution, he will eventually be credited with a £100 contribution because the balance of £23 will be reclaimed by the pension company from the Inland Revenue.

Higher rate tax payers who make FSAVCs find themselves in a slightly different position. They are entitled to tax relief at the rate of 40%. However, the pension company can only reclaim tax relief at the standard rate of 23%. The employee has to recover the additional 17% of tax relief by making a claim on his annual tax return.

Personal Pension Schemes

Personal Pension Plans are usually taken out by individuals who:

- either work for companies who do not have a company pension scheme, or
- don't want to join their employer's company pension scheme.

Generally, these employees contact a large pension company and make pension contributions directly to that pension company's fund. Personal Pension Scheme contributions are free of tax up to the following limits:

Age on 6 April	Max % of Net Relevant Earnings
35 or less	17½
36 - 45	20
46 - 50	25
51 - 55	30
56 - 60	35
61 - 74	40

For most employees, 'net relevant earnings' will be their gross salary plus the value of any benefits in kind. If the employee does not make the maximum contribution in any one year, they will have 'unused relief'. Unused relief is the difference between the maximum allowable and the level that has been contributed. It is possible to carry this unused relief forward for up to six years which means that the employee can make higher contributions in later years.

It is also possible to carry back a contribution for tax purposes up to the previous tax year. This means that the premium is treated as being paid in the previous tax year for tax purposes. This may save tax if, for example, the employee was a higher rate tax payer in the previous year but only a basic rate tax payer in the current year. By carrying back the premium to the previous year, the employee could obtain higher tax relief on the premium.

As you can see, the level of tax free contributions increases as the employee gets older. Notice that the funding limits are more generous than for occupational schemes which remain at 15%, irrespective of age.

Payroll Implications for Personal Pension Schemes

The payroll department has no responsibility for the administration of personal pension schemes. The responsibility for personal pensions rests entirely with the employee.

Members of personal pension plans are contracted out of SERPS which qualifies them for the lower rate of national insurance contributions. In practice, however, most plans arrange for national insurance deductions to be made at the (higher) contracted in rates. The difference in rates is periodically rebated to the pension scheme by the DSS. This is beneficial for the payroll administrator because it simplifies administration. Some employees could be contracted into the state scheme and some contracted out. Since the DSS have a record of who is contracted in and who is contracted out, it is easier for the payroll administrator to apply the higher rate of NICs to all employees and let DSS sort out the refunds.

Employees who have personal pension plans suffer tax deductions on the whole of their salary. Wages and salaries are calculated on the gross amount. However, the employee's tax relief is not lost. It is refunded to the pension company by the Inland Revenue.

Some employers *volunteer* to make contributions into an employee's personal pension plan. In this instance, employers will make a gross contribution and receive tax relief by including the premium in their accounts as an expense.

Further Reading on Pensions

The following Inland Revenue booklets may be useful:

IR76 Personal Pension Scheme - Guidance Notes

IR78 Personal Pensions - A guide for tax

IR120 You and the Pension Schemes Office

IR121 Income Tax and Pensioners

IR129 Occupational Pension Schemes - An introduction

PSO1 Occupational Pension Schemes - A guide for members of tax approved schemes

CWG2 Employers' Further Guide to PAYE and NICs

CWG1 Card 22 Changes to the working out of contracted out NICs resulting from the Pensions Act 1995.

National Insurance

National Insurance Contributions (NICs) are sums of money collected by Government based on employee's earnings. These contributions make employees eligible for state welfare benefits including:

- Unemployment benefit
- Sickness benefit
- Retirement pension
- Family credit
- Child benefit

etc.

National Insurance is administered by the Contributions Agency. Contributions are divided into four classes. These are:

Class 1 is a contribution levied on employed persons and their employers.

Class 1A is a special contribution paid by the *employer* over and above the Class 1 contribution which applies to the private use of cars and petrol.

Class 2 is a flat rate contribution levied on the self employed. The self employed normally have to pay Class 4 contributions as well.

Class 3 is a voluntary contribution which preserves entitlement to some contributory state benefits for those who are not making contributions via their work.

Class 4 is a profit related contribution paid by the self employed. It is paid in addition to their Class 2 contributions. The amount paid is dependent upon business profitability.

This book deals with the contributions relating to employment. These are Class 1 and Class 1A contributions. We will not deal with Class 2 and Class 4 contributions since these only relate to self employment.

Class 1 Contributions

There is a contributions threshold

Class 1 contributions are paid by employed persons and their employers. Every employed person has to contribute except:

- Employees on very low earnings
- Employees over state pension age.

The lower earnings limit between 6 April 1997 and 5 April 1998 is £62 per week. This means that neither the employee nor the employer has to make any NI contribution if the employee's wage remains below that level.

The state pension age for men is 65 and 60 for women. Although *employees* of pensionable age don't pay national insurance, their *employers* still have to contribute!

The level of National Insurance levied on Class 1 contributions depends on whether the employee is contracted into or out of SERPS. SERPS stands for 'State Earnings Related Pension Scheme'. SERPS is a graduated pension scheme run by the government. A graduated pension scheme is one where those who pay higher contributions during their working life enjoy higher pensions when they retire.

Employees do not have to be a member of SERPS. If an employer arranges a pension scheme for employees which is at least as good as SERPS then the employees can 'contract out' of the state scheme (in official parlance, people who are contracted out are called 'not contracted in'). The 'contracted out' scheme must be approved by the Pension Schemes Office. Contracted out employees are still entitled to a basic pension. This basic pension is topped up with payments from the private pension scheme arranged through the employer.

And a contributions ceiling

Employees who have spent part of their working lives contracted into SERPS and part of their working lives contracted into a private scheme are entitled to some SERPS pension. The amount of SERPS pension will depend on the contributions they have made whilst in SERPS. Normally they will top up their SERPS pension with an additional pension based on their contributions made to the private scheme.

Not surprisingly, those who are contracted into the state system have to pay higher contributions than those who are contracted out. This is because contracted out employees have to pay pension premiums to their private pension provider on top of their basic Class 1 contributions.

Class 1 National Insurance Rates

Above the lower earnings limit, both the employer and the employee have to pay national insurance contributions. The lower earnings limit for 1997/98 is:

- £62 per week, or
- £268 per month, or
- £3224 per annum.

For illustration purposes, we have used the weekly tables.

Contracted In Contributions

The contribution rates shown below apply to employees who are 'contracted into' SERPS. No national insurance is paid provided the employee earns less than £62 per week (1997/98). However, once the £62 per week threshold has been reached, employees' and employer's contributions are payable on the *whole* of the earnings.

Class 1 Rates Payable on All Earnings 1997/98

Earnings per week	Contracted In	
	Employer	Employee
£	%	%
62 - 109.99	3	*2/10**
110 - 154.99	5	*2/10**
155 - 209.99	7	*2/10**
210 - 465	10	*2/10**
over 465	10	£41.54

* on first £62

** on amounts over £62

For the employee, the tax on the first £62 of earnings is only 2%. However, earnings over £62 are taxed at 10% up to the upper earnings limit of £465. The upper earnings limit means that no contracted in employee pays more than £41.54 per week however much they earn.

The upper earnings limits for the employee are:

- £465 per week, which equates to
- £2015 per month, which equates to
- £24,180 per annum.

Note that there is no employer's ceiling. The employer has to pay Class 1 contributions on the whole of the earnings of the employee no matter how high the salary. For example, the employer's contribution based on an employee earning just £200 per week would be £200 @ 7% which is £14. On the other hand, the employer's national insurance contribution based on an employee who earns £1,000 per week would be £1000 @ 10% which is £100!

Not Contracted In Contributions

These tables apply where the employee is not contracted into SERPS. This means that the employee will be relying on the employer's pension scheme for the bulk of his/her pension. No national insurance is paid if the employee earns less than £62 per week. However, once this threshold is reached, similar rules apply as for 'contracted in' contributions. Here are the 'contracted out' rates.

Class 1 Rates Payable on All Earnings 1997/98

Earnings per week	Contracted Out	
	Employer	Employee
£	%	%
62 - 109.99	*3.0/0.0†	*2/8.4†
110 - 154.99	*5.0/2.0†	*2/8.4†
155 - 209.99	*7.0/4.0†	*2/8.4†
210 - 465	*10.0/7.0†	*2/8.4†
over 465	**10.0/7.0†	£35.09

* on first £62
** on first £62 and on earnings in excess of £465
† on earnings in excess of £62

Note that the rates are generally lower than for contracted in contributions. This is because the employee, and possibly the employer, are contributing to a private pension scheme. Note that the employee pays only 2% on the first £62 of earnings. Employees' earnings above £62 per week attract a tax rate of 8.4% subject to a maximum payment of £35.09 per week.

Contracted out national insurance tables are not generally available. They are issued to appropriate employers by the Contributions Agency each tax year. Contracted out rates and details are contained in leaflets CA39 and CA43.

Example

Here is an example for a 'contracted in' employee earning £500 per week.

Employee's contribution:

	£
First £62 @ 2%	1.24
Balance of £438 @ 10%	43.80
Total weekly contribution	45.04

But the maximum employee's contribution is limited to £41.54 so the employee's contribution in this case is £41.54.

Employer's contribution:

Employee's earnings	£500 per week
Contribution @ 10% =	£50 per week

Methods of Calculating Class 1 Contributions

Class 1 national insurance contributions can be:

- calculated by hand, or
- read from tables, or
- supplied automatically by a computerised payroll programme.

If you elect to calculate national insurance by hand, use a calculator and the rates shown in the appropriate table above. Fractions of a penny are rounded to the nearest whole penny.

Here are some notes on how to use the national insurance tables.

Using the National Insurance Tables

The government provides national insurance tables covering:

Contracted In Rates	Table A
Reduced Rates	Table B
Pensions Rates	Table C
Contracted Out Rates	Table D
Reduced Rates and Contracted Out	Table E

Each table is available in two parts. One is for weekly paid employees. The other is for monthly paid employees. Let's have a look at some of these tables.

Contracted In Rates - Table A

Table A (Standard Rate) is for employees who make standard rated contributions and who are not contracted out of SERPS. You will find Table A in the green National Insurance booklet CA38 from April 1997. Table A is available in a weekly and a monthly form. See the examples in Appendix 2 on pages 190 and 191. Notice that each table has four columns as follows:

Earnings on which employee's contributions payable 1a	Total of employee's and employer's contributions payable 1b	Employee's contributions payable 1c	▼ Employer's contributions

Headings 1a, 1b and 1c match the columns at the left hand side of the P11 (see page 69). This makes calculation of the employee's contribution very simple. Simply look up the employee's gross wage in the tables (ignoring the pence) and read off the contribution. Notice that the weekly tables start at the minimum level at which *employees* have to pay National Insurance, ie £62 for the tax year 1997/98, and finish at £465 which is the highest level at which an individual can contribute even if their weekly earnings exceed this amount. Remember, however, that the *employer* has to contribute over the whole of the earnings however high they may be.

Reduced Rates - Table B

Reduced rate applies to married women and widows who have the right to pay reduced rates of national insurance contributions in return for reduced national insurance benefits. Although the right to pay reduced rate contributions was lost in May 1977, a few married women and widows still pay reduced rate contributions because they continue to satisfy certain conditions. You cannot apply Table B unless a valid reduced rate certificate is produced. The layout of Table B is exactly the same as for Table A (see example on page 192). Notice, however, that the level of contribution is only 3.85% of earnings. Once again, there is a threshold below which no National Insurance is paid. If that threshold is exceeded, contributions are payable on the whole of the earnings. Notice again that there is a contribution ceiling for employees based on earnings of £465 per week.

Pension Rates - Table C

Table C is for employees over the state retirement age (60 for women and 65 for men). No contributions are due from the *employees* but the employer's national insurance contributions remain payable on the full earnings. You will notice that, in this case, there are only two columns 1a and 1b. As before, you simply read off the values in the relevant column and enter them onto the P11 for the appropriate week or month. Since these are employer's contributions, there is no ceiling on the amount of National Insurance levied.

National Insurance Tables!

Contracted Out Rates - Table D

Table D applies where employees are contracted out of SERPS. Table D appears in the green book of tables labelled 'Contracted Out Contributions', CA39 from April 1997. Table D has six columns labelled 1a, 1b, 1c, 1d, 1e and a column for employer's contributions. The readings from the columns are entered on the left hand side of form P11.

Beware! Some pension scheme deductions are made as if the pensions were contracted *into* SERPS. This means that the employee pays more national insurance than they should do. The extra national insurance contribution is remitted to the pension company by the Contributions Agency.

Contracted out Reduced Rates Contributions - Table E

Contribution rates for contracted out women who pay reduced rates are contained in Table E which is in the green Contributions Agency booklet 'Contracted Out Contributions' CA43. Once again, the tables comprise six columns labelled 1a, 1b, 1c, 1d, 1e and employer's contributions.

Exercise 3

Calculate Sally's Class 1 national insurance contributions between 6 April and 5 September. Remember her earnings were:

	£
April	1100
May	1200
June	1400
July	1250
Aug	1500

Enter your answer on Sally's P11 which is found on pages 69 and 70. Ignore Class 1A contributions. Use the tables on pages 190 to 191.

Check your answer with page 200.

Paying Over Class I National Insurance Contributions

Class 1 national insurance contributions are collected via the 'Pay As You Earn' system. This means that the Inland Revenue acts as a tax collector for the Contributions Agency.

First you need to calculate how much tax and national insurance is due for each employee. Add up all of the tax and national insurance contributions for all your employees for each tax month. Remember, a tax month ends on the fifth of each month. You have to pay the tax and NIC collections to the Inland Revenue Accounts Office within 14 days of each tax month end. Since the tax month ends on the fifth, that means you must make your payments by the 19th of each month.

Send in a payslip with your payment. You are supplied with payslips in a payslip booklet. An example of a payslip (P30B) is shown on page 46. Payment should be made to the Collector of Taxes, Accounts Office Shipley, Bradford, West Yorkshire, BD98 8AA. Payment can be made by bank giro, Girobank transfer, at a Post Office, by BACS, or by post.

If you keep a record of your monthly payments, you will find it easier to complete your year end documentation. We suggest you keep this record either in the payslip booklet or on a special form provided by the Inland Revenue, form P32. Examples are shown on pages 46 and 47.

Class 1A Contributions

Class 1A national insurance is a tax on employers who allow their employees to use business cars for private use. The contribution applies where an employee:

- is a director or an employee earning more than £8500 per annum, who
- has the use of a company car, and
- has private use of that vehicle.

The tax is paid as a lump sum on 19 July each year based on the car benefit enjoyed by employees during the previous tax year. Calculations are based on both:

- Car benefit, and
- Fuel scale charges.

Let's have a look at those two benefits in a little more detail.

Car Benefit

The value of car benefit for national insurance purposes is the same value as that for Income Tax purposes (we looked at this in Section 9 - Expenses and Benefits). Car benefit is calculated as 35% of the original list price of the car plus any additional accessories. The original list price will apply irrespective of whether the car was bought with a discount or even second-hand.

Where an employee is required to contribute towards the cost of purchasing the car, a deduction can be made from the original list price up to a maximum of £5,000. This will reduce the value on which the benefit is based. The maximum list price applicable to vehicles is currently £80,000. Any vehicle costing more than £80,000 is deemed to have a benefit value of £80,000 only. There are special rules for cars which are 15 years old or more.

Car benefit charges are reduced as follows:

- If the employee drives more than 2,500 business miles per year then the benefit is reduced by one third.

- If the employee drives more than 18,000 business miles per year then the benefit is reduced by two thirds.

- There is a further one third reduction from this residual figure if the car is over four years old at the beginning of the tax year.

Since the benefit depends on the amount of business mileage, the employee should keep a mileage log. This will need to be produced if the DSS decide to check the level of Class 1A national insurance contributions.

Let's consider an example.

Example

Sally's company car had an original list price of £10,000 and had additional accessories of £2,000 fitted. Sally completes 20,000 business miles a year and the car was over four years old on 5 April 1997. The benefit would be calculated as follows:

	£	£
List Price of Car	10000	
Accessories	2000	
Total Cost	12000	
Car Benefit is £12000 x 35%		4200
Less Discount for High Mileage 2/3		(2800)
		1400
Less Discount for Age 1/3		(467)
Amount of Benefit		933

The value of car benefit can be further reduced if the car is not available for a complete year. The reduction is proportional to the number of days of non availability expressed as a fraction of 365. Employees' payments for private use also reduce the benefit on a pound for pound basis.

We will see how to calculate the Class 1A national insurance contributions due on car benefit after looking at fuel benefit.

Fuel Benefit

Fuel benefit applies where an employee is provided with fuel for private use. Fuel benefit scale charges are added to the car benefit when working out Class 1A contributions.

For 1997/98, annual fuel benefit scale charges were as follows.

PETROL		DIESEL	
Engine Size	**Scale Charge**	**Engine Size**	**Scale Charge**
	£		£
0 - 1400 cc	800		
1401-2000 cc	1010	0 - 2000 cc	740
2001 cc +	1490	2001 cc +	940

Remember that the Class 1 national insurance contributions paid by 19 July 1998 are based on car usage between 6 April 1997 and 5 April 1998.

The employer has to pay the Class 1A national insurance contributions shown in the table, irrespective of the amount of private mileage undertaken by the employee.

How to Work Out Class 1A Car and Fuel Contributions

Once we have worked out the benefit in kind on the car and the fuel benefit, we can go on to work out the Class 1A contributions payable on Sally's car for 1997/98 assuming:

- Sally is provided with fuel for private use
- The car is a petrol vehicle with a 1600 cc engine.

The rate of Class 1A contributions for cars made available in the 1997/98 tax year is 10%.

	£
Sally's Car Benefit	933
Add Fuel Benefit	1010
Total Benefits	1943

Class 1A Contribution = 1943 x 10% = £194.30

Class 1A contributions do not relate to trucks, vans or lorries but they do relate to estate cars, Range Rovers etc.

There are a host of adjustments which can be made to the national insurance contributions payable. These include adjustments for the number of days the cars were available for private use, shared cars, pooled cars, disabled drivers etc. Check the Contributions Agency booklet CA33 from April 1996 (and supplement April 1997) entitled 'Cars and Fuel - Manual for Employers'.

Table Y doesn't exist!

Completing the P14

At the end of the tax year, the employer will need to add the Class 1A contribution to the P14 Annual Summary (see example below). Label the car and fuel benefit table as 'Table Y'.

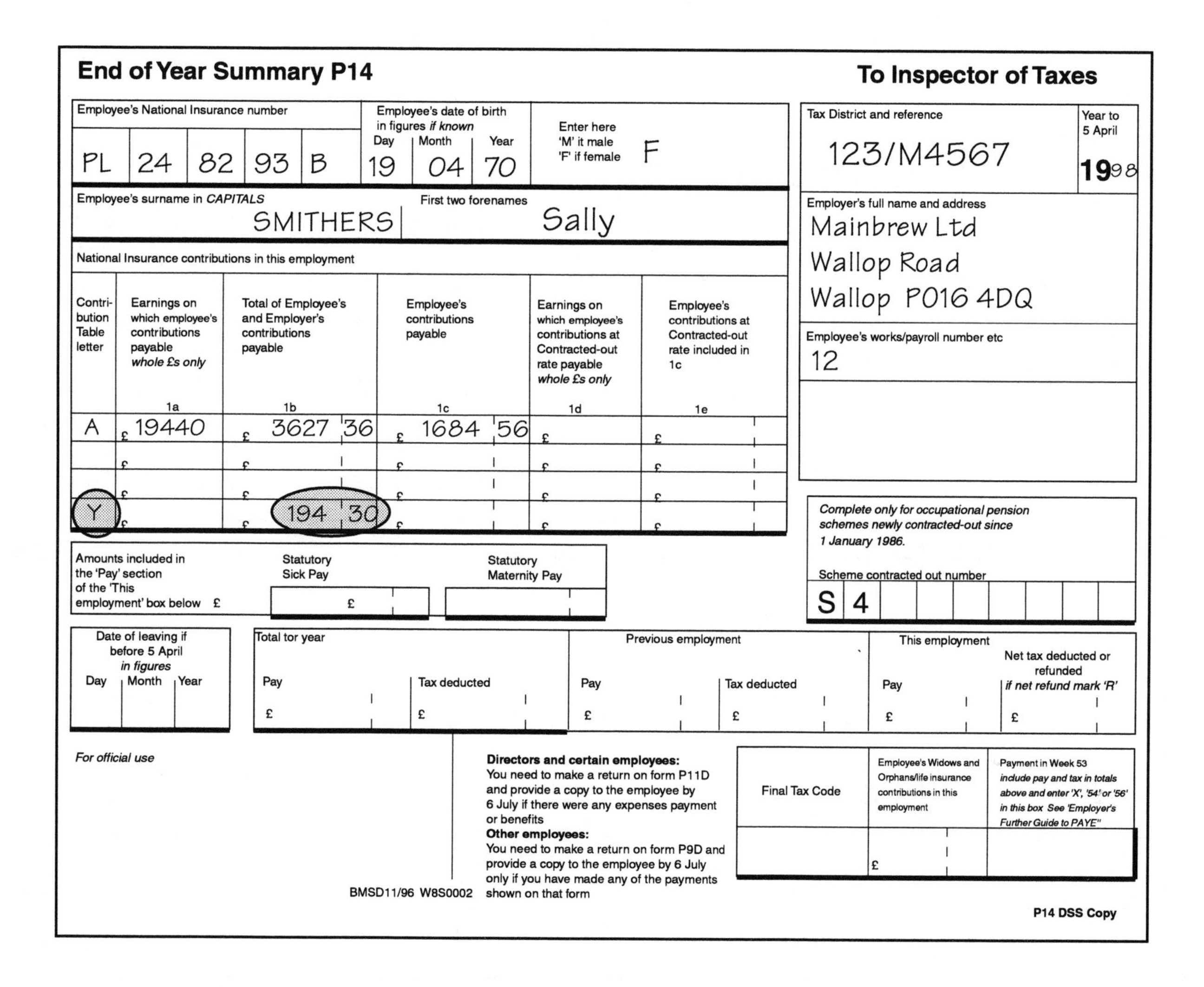

End of Year Summary P14 **To Inspector of Taxes**

Employee's National Insurance number: PL 24 82 93 B

Employee's date of birth in figures *if known* — Day: 19 Month: 04 Year: 70

Enter here 'M' if male 'F' if female: F

Tax District and reference: 123/M4567

Year to 5 April: 1998

Employee's surname in *CAPITALS*: SMITHERS — First two forenames: Sally

Employer's full name and address: Mainbrew Ltd, Wallop Road, Wallop PO16 4DQ

Employee's works/payroll number etc: 12

National Insurance contributions in this employment

Contribution Table letter	Earnings on which employee's contributions payable *whole £s only* (1a)	Total of Employee's and Employer's contributions payable (1b)	Employee's contributions payable (1c)	Earnings on which employee's contributions at Contracted-out rate payable *whole £s only* (1d)	Employee's contributions at Contracted-out rate included in 1c (1e)
A	£ 19440	£ 3627.36	£ 1684.56	£	£
	£	£	£	£	£
	£	£	£	£	£
Y	£	£ 194.30	£	£	£

Amounts included in the 'Pay' section of the 'This employment' box below £ — Statutory Sick Pay £ — Statutory Maternity Pay

Complete only for occupational pension schemes newly contracted-out since 1 January 1986.

Scheme contracted out number: S 4

Date of leaving if before 5 April *in figures* — Day / Month / Year

Total tor year — Pay £ — Tax deducted £

Previous employment — Pay £ — Tax deducted £

This employment — Pay £ — Net tax deducted or refunded *if net refund mark 'R'* £

For official use

Directors and certain employees: You need to make a return on form P11D and provide a copy to the employee by 6 July if there were any expenses payment or benefits
Other employees: You need to make a return on form P9D and provide a copy to the employee by 6 July only if you have made any of the payments shown on that form

Final Tax Code

Employee's Widows and Orphans/life insurance contributions in this employment £

Payment in Week 53 *include pay and tax in totals above and enter 'X', '54' or '56' in this box See 'Employer's Further Guide to PAYE'*

BMSD11/96 W8S0002

P14 DSS Copy

Completing the P35 and P11

At the end of the tax year, the employer will also need to add the Class 1A contribution to the P11 and P35 forms (see examples on pages 146 and 147).

Remember, Class 1A contributions are paid annually in arrears. Contributions must be paid by 19 July each year for car related benefits enjoyed during the previous tax year. Contributions for all employees should be added to the June National Insurance calculation (which is also due on 19 July). This means that the 1997/98 payment is due by 19 July 1998. If the employer pays quarterly, payment is also due on 19 July.

Sally Smither's P11

Deductions Working Sheet P11 Year to 5 April 19 97

Employer's name Mainbrew Ltd

Tax Office and reference 123/M4567

National Insurance contributions

Earnings recorded in column 1a should not exceed the Upper Earnings Limit

For employer's use	Earnings on which employee's contributions payable *Whole pounds only* 1a	Total of employee's and employer's contributions payable 1b £	Employee's contribution payable 1c £	Earnings on which employee's contributions at contracted-out rate payable included in col. 1a *Whole pounds only* 1d £	Employee's contributions at contracted-out rate included in column 1c 1e £	Statutory Sick Pay in the week or month included in column 2 1f £	Statutory Maternity Pay in the week or month included in column 2 1g £	Statutory Maternity Pay recovered 1h £	Month no	Week no
	Bt fwd 11340	Bt fwd 2115 96	Bt fwd 982 66	Bt fwd	Bt fwd	Bt fwd	Bt fwd	Bt fwd	Bt fwd Mth 7	Bt fwd wk 30
										31
										32
										33
										34
	1620	302 28	140 38						8	35
										36
										37
										38
	1620	302 28	140 38						9	39
										40
										41
										42
	1620	302 28	140 38						10	43
										44
										45
										46
	1620	302 28	140 38						11	47
										48
										49
										50
										51
	1620	302 28	140 38						12	52
										§

SSP total SMP total

Don't look for Table Y - it doesn't exist!

Enter Class 1A contributions here

Enter the NI Contribution Table Letter here

End of Year Summary

Table letter	1a	1b	1c	1d	1e
A	19440	3627.36	1684.56		
Y		194.30			

Scheme Contracted-Out Numbers
(For Contracted-Out Purchase Schemes only)

S	
S	
S	
S	

P11(1997)

Example P35

Add together the year's Class 1 contributions to the annual Class 1A contribution

Deductions Working Sheets

List here the individual *Deductions Working Sheets* (forms P11) which you have filled in during the year and which contain a figure under either of the headings shown.

If there is not enough space here to list all your employees please prepare continuation sheets.

Employee's name Put an asterisk (*) beside the name if the person is a director	**National Insurance contributions (NIC)** Enter the total of the employee's and employer's NIC †	*Enter only the figures for 'this employment'* **Income tax deducted or refunded** Write 'R' beside amount to show a net refund
W Gates	£ 3812 . 31	£
	£	£
	£	£
	£	£
	£	£
	£	£
	£	£
	£	£
	£	£
	£	£
	£	£
	£	£
	£	£

† Include Class 1A contributions payable in the year, unless you paid these by the Alternative Payment Method.

Note: the columns for **SSP and SMP paid** have been discontinued, but the figures may still appear on some computer-printed continuation sheets. If so, please ignore them.

Calculation of NIC and Income Tax now due

National Insurance contributions (NIC)

Total from this page	A	£ 3812 . 31
Total from continuation sheets	B	£
Total NIC A + B	C	£ 3812 . 31
Received from Inland Revenue to pay SSP / SMP	D	£
C + D	E	£ 3812 . 31
Statutory Sick Pay **recovered**	F	£
Statutory MaternityPay **recovered**	G	£
NIC compensation on SMP see your payment record	H	£
NIC Holiday claimed	I	£
F + G + H + I	J	£
Total NIC payable to Accounts Office E - J	K	£ 3812 . 31
NIC already paid	L	£ 3812 . 31
NIC now due K - L	M	£ Nil

Remember to deduct amounts marked "R"

Income Tax

Total from this page	N	
Total from continuation sheets	O	
Total tax N + O	P	
Received from Inland Revenue to refund tax	Q	£
Tax deducted from sub-contractors see your *Contractor's Statement* (form SC35)	R	£
P + Q + R	S	£
Tax already paid	T	£
Tax now due S - T	U	£

Do not send Payment with this form. Send it to the Inland Revenue Accounts Office immediately. See notes overleaf.

Contracted-out pension schemes

Enter here your employer's contracting-out number, where applicable:

(You will find the number on the Occupational Pensions Board's Certificate)

§ I claim payment under Section 7 of the Social Security Act 1986 for each employee on whose *End of Year Summary* (form P14) I have entered a scheme contracting-out number. So far as I know, none of these employees is in an employment which has been contracted-out by reference to any other scheme since 1 January 1986. "✓"

§ You can only claim if this form is used for 1992-93 or earlier

Class 1A Contributions for Leavers

The employer must create a P11 even if an employee leaves during a tax year. This is used to calculate the Class 1A contribution payable by the employer for the following year.

For example, if an employee leaves during the 1997/98 tax year, a P11 must be created for the 1998/99 tax year to reflect the payment in July 1998. A P11 should be completed for every employee even if the employee was no longer employed by the business at the end of the tax year. In the case of a leaver, the only entry on the P11 would be the entry for Class 1A national insurance shown under Table Y. The leaver's payment of the Class 1A contribution would also need to be recorded on the 1998/99 end of year return form P35.

Contributions Agency booklet CA33 from April 1996 called Cars and Fuel - Manual for Employers (and supplement April 1997) is available for further details.

Exercise 4

How much Class 1A contribution would an employer have to pay for an employee who had the following in the 1997/98 tax year?

- a five year old car
- original price £11,250
- engine capacity 1800cc
- driven by petrol
- covering 26,000 miles per annum.

Check your answer with page 201.

Section 13

Statutory Sick Pay

Introduction

Everyone suffers from ill health at some time or another. If the illness is severe enough, the employee may be unable to attend work. In the bad old days, no work meant no pay. However, in today's enlightened times, most employers continue to pay their employees when they are sick. The amount and duration of sickness pay should be documented in the employee's Contract of Employment.

However, some employers do not have sick pay schemes. To protect workers, the government sets a minimum entitlement to sickness pay called Statutory Sick Pay (SSP). SSP is a safety net of minimum sickness payments. Although the rules are set by government, the scheme is operated and paid for by the employer. The employer has no automatic right to reclaim SSP from government.

Under certain circumstances, however, the employer may be able to reclaim *part* of the SSP payments under the percentage threshold scheme which is explained later in this section.

Who is Entitled to Statutory Sick Pay?

SSP only applies to employees, it doesn't apply to self employed people. Be sure to distinguish between employed staff and self employed contractors! SSP is payable to:

- All employees under 65 who are sick for four or more days (including Saturdays, Sundays and Bank Holidays).

- Employees who make Class 1 national insurance contributions.

- Employees who do not earn enough to pay Class 1 contributions but would qualify if they earned enough.

- Part-time, temporary or casual employees are entitled to SSP in the same way as everyone else.

- There are special rules for mariners, armed services personnel, aircrew, continental shelf workers and employees of National Health Service Trusts. Check the Statutory Sick Pay Manual for Employers, CA30 from April 1997 for details.

Who is Not Entitled to Statutory Sick Pay?

The following people are not entitled to SSP:

- People in prison or those kept in custody by the police.

- People who work outside the European Economic area.

- People in receipt of Statutory Maternity Pay. People receiving Maternity *Allowance* from the DSS are not generally entitled to SSP for the 18 week period they are drawing the allowance.

- Employees over the age of 65.

- Employees engaged in a trade dispute.

- Employees who have been hired to work for the business but who have not yet commenced work.

- Agency workers are not normally entitled to SSP because their contracts usually end when they are not available for work.

No SSP in prison!

How does Statutory Sick Pay Work?

In order to understand SSP, we need to get to grips with a few terms. These are:

Period of Incapacity for Work

A 'period of incapacity for work' (PIW) is a period of sickness lasting for four days in a row. All days count including Saturdays, Sundays, bank holidays etc. To be eligible for SSP, an employee must be sick for four days or more in a row. Lesser periods of sickness make the employee ineligible for SSP.

Waiting Days

Even if an employee is sick for four or more days in a row, he will not necessarily be paid for every day's sickness. To begin with, SSP is only payable for normal working days (which are Monday to Friday for most people). Even then, the first three working days of sickness do not count for payment of SSP. These days are called 'waiting days'. Payment will commence on the fourth day of sickness provided that day is a normal working day.

Here is an example showing how 'waiting days' and 'period of incapacity for work' operate.

Example

An employee has a normal working week from Monday to Friday. He falls ill on a Saturday and returns to work on the following Thursday.

1 The period of sickness exceeds four days and, therefore, the rules of SSP apply.

2 Monday, Tuesday and Wednesday are working days. However, they are not 'paid' days because the first three working days are waiting days which are not paid for.

3 Since the employee returns to work on the Thursday, he is not entitled to be paid SSP.

Qualifying Days

Once a person has established their right to SSP, they are paid for days when they would normally work. For example, people who work Monday to Friday have five qualifying days in a week. This means that, in a full working week, they will receive payment of £55.70. If they only qualify for payment on two days of the week, they will be paid two fifths of £55.70 which is £22.28. Publication CA35/36 from April 1997, Statutory Sick Pay and Statutory Maternity Pay Tables contains a valuable table which is reproduced below.

Statutory Sick Pay Daily Rates Table

Unrounded daily rates	No of QDs in week	1	2	3	4	5	6	7
£		£	£	£	£	£	£	£
7.9571	7	7.96	15.92	23.88	31.83	39.79	47.75	55.70
9.2833	6	9.29	18.57	27.85	37.14	46.42	55.70	
11.1400	5	11.14	22.28	33.42	44.56	55.70		
13.9250	4	13.93	27.85	41.78	55.70			
18.5667	3	18.57	37.14	55.70				
27.8500	2	27.85	55.70					
54.7000	1	55.70						

Unrounded rates are included for employers with computerised payroll systems

To use the table, look up the number of days in a week that an employee normally works in the column labelled 'No of QDs in a Week' and then read across for the number of days which qualify for sickness pay. The point where the two intersect gives the sickness pay due to the employee for that week. For example, if an employee normally works four days a week and is due sickness pay for two qualifying days then he/she is due sickness pay of £27.85.

The table does reveal, rather surprisingly, that an employee who normally works one day a week is entitled to the full £55.70 if they are sick on their working day. However, an employee who normally works seven days a week only gets paid £7.96 for a single day's sickness!

Recurrent Sickness

Employees who have recurring sickness are subject to special rules. If they have two periods of sickness which are separated by eight weeks or less, they can be paid for the first three days of sickness when they become ill for the second time. The periods are 'linked' for the purpose of deciding when SSP is payable.

The DSS publication CA35/36 from April 1997 contains a very useful set of tables for 'linking' periods of incapacity for work.

Rates and Duration of Pay

For employees with average weekly earnings of £62 or more, a single weekly rate of SSP is payable. From 6 April 1997, this rate was set at £55.70.

SSP is payable for up to 28 weeks of sickness. The gross amount of SSP is subject to PAYE income tax deductions and National Insurance Contributions.

Of course, the employer is not bound to pay the *minimum* amount under the rules of SSP. The employer is free to top up the level of sickness pay to whatever level he chooses.

Forms used to Administer SSP

DSS provides several forms which are designed to help administer SSP. These are:

Form SC2 (part reproduced on page 158) is called the Employee's Statement of Sickness. It is optional but lists the kind of information you will need if your employee is sick for seven days or less. It is worth getting hold of a supply of these forms because:

- they are free
- they give useful background information for the employee
- they contain exactly what you need to know from your employee.

Form SSP1 is a 36 page booklet which you give to employees who are not eligible for SSP. The cover of this booklet is reproduced on page 159. Section 1 explains why the employee cannot receive SSP. Sections 2 and 3 comprise a claim for Incapacity Benefit for your employee to complete and submit to his local Social Security office.

Form SSP1(L) is the leaver's Statement of Statutory Sick Pay. The cover is reproduced on page 160. This is given to employees who are leaving you and have been paid SSP in the last eight weeks. This form helps people going to work for a new employer or claiming Incapacity Benefit since it establishes their last period of SSP.

Form SSP2 (see page 161) is a record sheet which will help the employer record all details required by law.

Form SSP33 (see page 162) is a checklist and worksheet. It tells you how to pay, record and reclaim SSP. It is used in conjunction with form SSP2.

These forms are available from your local Social Security Office.

Period of Incapacity for Work!

The Percentage Threshold Scheme

Under certain circumstances, employers may be able to recover a proportion of SSP paid. Recoveries would be made under the percentage threshold scheme. The amount that can be reclaimed is any balance of SSP in excess of 13% of total employer's and employees' National Insurance payments during each month (excluding Class 1A contributions). For example, in June:

Total Class 1 NIC liability	£856.25
13% of £856.25 =	£111.31
Total SSP payments	£149.29
Amount recoverable	£37.98 (£149.29 - £111.31)

SSP is recovered by withholding part of the NI contributions which are normally paid to government. Where the SSP recoverable exceeds NI contributions due for a month, any surplus is deducted as follows:

- from PAYE tax payments made in the month
- carried forward and deducted from the next payment period
- reclaimed from the Collector of Taxes on application.

Freedom from Operating Statutory Sick Pay

From 6 April 1997, employers who have sick pay schemes which pay above the statutory minimum of £55.70 per week can choose not to operate SSP if they choose to do so. There are conditions attached which are given on pages 9 and 10 of the Statutory Sick Pay Manual CA30 from April 1997. You can still recover any SSP due to you under the percentage threshold scheme even if you don't operate the Statutory Sick Pay Scheme.

Statutory Sick Pay Summary

- Tell employees that they must notify you *verbally* if they are sick for 1-3 days.
- If they are sick for more than 3 days but less than 7 days, ask them to notify you *in writing*. They can either use form SC2 or a similar form of your own devising which contains the same information.
- If they are off work for more than 7 days, tell them to get a sick note from their *doctor*.
- If your employee is sick for 4 or more days in a row, he is entitled to SSP (subject to meeting the conditions outlined on pages 149 and 150).
- Statutory Sick Pay is payable for days when an employee normally works for you. For most employees, this is from Monday to Friday.
- To calculate the SSP payable, look up the table on page 3 of the Statutory Sick Pay and Statutory Maternity Pay Tables (booklet CA35/36 from April 1997), reproduced in this book on page 194. Look at the second column which is labelled 'No of QDs in week'. This column represents the number of days which qualify for sick payments. Read across the row for the number of days that the person was actually sick. The point of the intersection shows the employee's entitlement to SSP (see example overleaf).

  If you don't want to look up a table, you can calculate the daily rate for yourself or use the precalculated daily rates shown in column 1 which are rounded to 4 decimal places.

- Enter the amount of sick pay on the person's P11D and calculate tax and national insurance in the usual way.

Be sure to have a look at form SSP33 which contains a handy checklist and worksheet for paying SSP.

Let's look at an example using the table on page 194.

Example

John has average weekly earnings of £235 and works for you from Monday to Friday. John is away sick from Sunday to the following Sunday. We will assume that there are no previous PIWs in the preceding eight weeks.

The first three qualifying days will be waiting days and Statutory Sick Pay will not be payable for these days. Therefore, Statutory Sick Pay will only be payable for Thursday and Friday, remembering that Statutory Sick Pay will not be payable for Saturday and Sunday as these are not qualifying days in John's case.

We would now refer to the table providing the daily rates of SSP payable. We would then find the number of qualifying days in the week. John has five so we would find (5) in the 'number of qualifying days in a week' column. We have decided that Statutory Sick Pay is payable for two days so we would then move across to the column headed by (2). This gives us an amount of Statutory Sick Pay payable of £22.28. This would then be treated as earnings during the week and we would then calculate PAYE and National Insurance as per normal using the form P11.

Have a go at the following exercise yourself.

Exercise 5

Using the tables on page 194, compute the Statutory Sick Pay payable for the following employees.

Assume that there are no linking PIWs in the previous eight weeks.

Employee	Average Weekly Earnings £	No of Qualifying Days in Week	Days Sick	SSP Payable in Week £
Jan	220	6	Sunday to Friday	
Joe	199	5	Sunday to Sunday	
Stuart	56	5	Tuesday to Friday	
Donna	136	4	Monday to Wednesday	

Check your answer with page 201.

Need to Know More?

SSP is a complicated scheme which needs an 84 page manual to explain it. The official guides are:

- Statutory Sick Pay Manual for Employers CA30 from April 1997
- Statutory Sick Pay and Statutory Maternity Pay Tables CA35/36 from April 1997
- Card 16 of the Employers' Quick Guide to PAYE and National Insurance Contributions CWG1.

Inside Pages of Form SC2

Employee's statement of sickness - continued

If you go abroad

If you are sick
on or after 6 April 1996, **and**
there is more than 8 weeks between this spell of sickness and an earlier spell which started before 6 April 1996, **and**
you are outside the European Economic Area (EEA), **and**
your employer is liable to pay Class 1 National Insurance contributions
you may be able to get SSP if you meet the other conditions for entitlement.

If you are sick
before 6 April 1996, **or**
after 6 April 1996 but there is 8 weeks or less between this spell of sickness and an earlier spell which started before 6 April 1996, **and**
you are outside the EEA
you will not be entitled to SSP

You can find out more about this in leaflet **NI 244** *Statutory Sick Pay - Check your rights.*

Other help while you are sick

You can get more information about other help while you are sick in leaflet **FB 28** *Sick or disabled?.*

If you do not have much money coming in while you are sick, you may be able to get Income Support. Income Support is a social security benefit for people who do not have enough money to live on. You can find out more about Income Support in leaflet **IS 1** from
any social security office
most advice centres like the Citizens Advice Bureau
any post office

If you want to know more about SSP or other help while you are sick, ring Freeline Social Security. The phone call is free. The number is **0800 666 555.**

Your statement

About you

Surname

Other names

Title

National Insurance (NI) number

Date of birth / /

Clock or payroll number

About your sickness

Please give brief details of your sickness

What date did your sickness begin? / /

What date did your sickness end? / /
If you do not know when your sickness will end, leave this box blank.

The dates you put in these 2 boxes may be days you do not normally work.
If you are sick for more than 7 days, your employer may ask you for a medical certificate. Medical certificates are also called sick notes or doctor's statements.

Was your sickness caused by an accident at work or an industrial disease?
No
Yes You may be able to get Industrial Injuries Disablement Benefit. If you want to claim this, please get in touch with your local social security office.

Your signature

Your signature

Date / /

Tear off this page and give it to your employer.

Cover of 36 page Booklet on SSP

SSP 1 (Apr 96)

Statutory Sick Pay (SSP) and Incapacity Benefit

Claim form

About this form

There are **4** sections in this form.

Section 1
is for the employer to give information about Statutory Sick Pay (SSP). Notes for the employer about when to fill in this form are on **page 2** of this form.

Section 2, 3 and **4**
are for the employee to claim Incapacity Benefit.

Statutory Sick Pay is money paid by employers to employees who are away from work for 4 days or more in a row because they are sick.

Incapacity Benefit is a social security benefit you may be able to get if you are still sick when your SSP ends or if you cannot get SSP.

Section 1

About SSP and your employee

About your employee

Please tell us about your employee

Surname ____________________

Other names ____________________

National Insurance (NI) number Letters | Numbers | Letter
☐☐ ☐☐ ☐☐ ☐☐ ☐

Clock or payroll number ____________________

Tax reference number ____________________

Use this Form only for Leavers

SSP 1(L)

Leaver's statement of Statutory Sick Pay (SSP)

About this form

There are **2** sections in this form.
Section 1 is for the employer to give information about Statutory Sick Pay (SSP) and their employee.
Section 2 contains information for the employee.

Section 1

Notes to the employer

Who to use this form for

Use this form for anyone who

- asks for the form, and
- is not going to work for you any more or who has already finished working for you, and
- has been paid SSP in the last 8 weeks that they worked for you, and
- has been paid SSP for one week or more. Remember odd days can be rounded up, see **About SSP** on the **next page.**

About your employee

Please tell us about your employee

Surname ______

Other names ______

National Insurance (NI) number Letters ☐☐ Numbers ☐☐ ☐☐ ☐☐ Letter ☐

Clock or payroll number ______

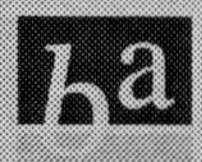

An Executive Agency of the Department of Social Security

Reproduction of Part of Form SSP2

Statutory Sick Pay record sheet
Form SSP2

Employee's full name	
Tax year	/

Information brought forward			
A First day of PIW	/ /	**D** Waiting days in PIW with you	1 ☐
B Date SSP1 change-over Form issued	/ /		2 ☐
C Last day of PIW	/ /		3 ☐

1 Tick the qualifying days Sun	Mon	Tue	Wed	Thu	Fri	Sat	Date
☐	☐	☐	☐	☐	☐	☐	/ /
☐	☐	☐	☐	☐	☐	☐	/ /
☐	☐	☐	☐	☐	☐	☐	/ /

	£	£	£	£	£	£	£

Week ending Saturday	Week	**3** Record of sickness and SSP Sun	Mon	Tue	Wed	Thu	Fri	Sat	**4** SSP due in week/month	**5** Running total of SSP	**6** Remarks
	27										
	28										
	29										
	30										
	31										
	32										
	33										
	34										
	35										
	36										
	37										
	38										
	39										
	40										
	41										
	42										
	43										
	44										
	45										
	46										
	47										
	48										
	49										
	50										
	51										
	52										
	*										

How to use this Statutory Sick Pay (SSP) record sheet

This record sheet is for the basic sickness records that you must keep for the SSP scheme. You do not have to use this record sheet. You can keep the extra records.

Boxes A - D - Information brought forward

Take the information from the previous years records. For new employee's use the Leaver's Statement - Form SSP1(L) for boxes A and C, if appropriate.

Boxes 1-3

Box 1 Tick the qualifying days, and write in the date of any change.

Box 2 Write in the maximum liability.
Remember that you have to pay 28 weeks in a Period of Incapacity for Work (PIW). But if linked PIW's with you run longer than 3 years, your liability stops.

Box 3 Use the following code letters to note the days of sickness:

- W Waiting days.
- N Non-qualifying days.
- C Change over days for which SSP is not due. Give the reasons in Box 6. Remember to issue Change-over Form SSP1.
- X Sickness in doubt, or late notification. Give the reasons in Box 6.
- P SSP is due. Only use **'P'** where the qualifying days vary. **If they do not vary,** write in the numbers. Always note 4 days or more of sickness, whether or not SSP is due.

If the qualifying days are the same each week:

- Use the **'days'** parts of Box 2
- Note the days of SSP due in numbers. Write 1, 2, 3, 4, 5 etc in Box 3
- If the qualifying days change, write the new details in Boxes 1 and 2

If the qualifying days are not the same each week:

- Use the **'money'** parts of Box 2
- Write **'P'** in Box 3 for each day SSP is due
- Keep a running total of SSP in Box 5

At the beginning of a new tax year, start a new record sheet. Write in any new details for Box 2.

If a new employee gives you a Leaver's Statement, Form SSP1(L), that can be used, add it's information to Box 2.

If SSP is due after a gap of more than 8 weeks, work out new details for Box 2.

For more information see the 'Employers Manual' on Statutory Sick Pay, Leaflet CA30(NI270).

* Use the last line if sickness at the end of the tax year includes part of the 53rd week.

Cover of Form SSP33
(Inside pages of form contain useful checklist and worksheet)

SSP **Statutory Sick Pay** **Form SSP33**

Checklist and worksheet

Part 1 is a self-certificate form for your employee's use. Part 2 is a checklist to guide you through the steps you must take to pay, record and get back Statutory Sick Pay (SSP).

What to do

Use the checklist as a worksheet by filling in the answer spaces as you go.

You will also need:

- form SSP2 of your own SSP record form
- SSP Tables, CA35(SSP55)
- Quick Guide, CA27(NI268)
- SSP Manual, CA30(NI270)

Part 1 - to be completed by the employee

Full name

National Insurance Number — Letters / Numbers / Letter

Clock or payroll number

Reasons for absence

First day of sickness — Day / Month / Year: / /

Did you do any work on that day? **Yes** ☐ **No** ☐

Last day of sickness — Day / Month / Year: / /

Did you see your doctor or go to hospital? **Yes** ☐ **No** ☐

If **Yes**, did you get a sick note? **Yes** ☐ **No** ☐

Signature

Date / /

Part 2 - to be completed by the employer

Notification and evidence of incapacity

1	If notification is made later than your rules specify, or later than the 7th calendar day, and you consider there was no 'good cause' for delay, you can withhold SSP. See paragraph 23 of CA30(NI270)	**Was notification in time?**	**Yes** ☐ Go to step **2** **No** ☐ How many days SSP are you withholding?
2	If you believe the incapacity is not genuine, you can refuse to pay SSP. See paragraph 27 of CA30(NI270).	**Do you believe the incapacity is genuine?**	**Yes** ☐ Go to step **3** **No** ☐ Tell your employee why you will not be paying them SSP.

Please turn over ▶

Section 14

Statutory Maternity Pay

Introduction

In broad outline, Statutory Maternity Pay is paid to pregnant employees provided that they:

- Have worked for you for at least 26 weeks
- Earn enough to pay Class 1 National Insurance
- Stop work to have their babies
- Give you medical evidence of when the baby is due (eg a doctor's note)
- Are still pregnant 11 weeks before the baby is due
- Give you three week's notice before they take their maternity leave.

If your employee looks as if she meets these conditions then you need to read on.

Description of Statutory Maternity Pay

Statutory Maternity Pay (SMP) sets minimum payments to women who stop work to have a baby. The scheme is administered by the employer. However, most of the costs are borne by the government as follows.

- Small employers can recover 100% of SMP plus 6.5% additional compensation to cover the NI contributions paid on the SMP. A small employer is defined as one whose gross Class 1 NI contributions (excluding Class 1A) were £20,000 or less in the previous tax year.

- Large employers can recover 92% of the SMP paid out.

The employer is reimbursed by withholding money from the monthly National Insurance and PAYE payments to the Collector of Taxes. Very small employers may not collect enough NI and PAYE to meet the SMP bill. In this case, the employer can reclaim SMP direct from the Inland Revenue Accounts Office.

SMP sets minimum payments to pregnant employees. The employer is free to top up these minimum payments to whatever level he chooses. Statutory Maternity Pay is payable at:

- 90% of the employee's average weekly earnings for the first six weeks, subject to a minimum payment of £55.70 per week.

- £55.70 for the rest of the maternity period.

The maximum maternity period is 18 weeks. The employer is free to pay the employee by any method he chooses. In general, SMP is paid in the same way as normal pay. It is subject to NI and PAYE deductions.

These notes relate to the rules in England, Wales and Scotland. There are slight differences to the scheme in Northern Ireland. Special rules apply to:

- Mariners
- Employees who work outside the European Economic Area
- Employees who work for more than one employer at the same time
- Employees with two or more employments with the same employer
- Employees working for National Health Service Trusts.

If you have any employees who are covered by these rules, consult the Statutory Maternity Pay Manual CA29 from April 1997.

Administering Statutory Maternity Pay

In order to administer the scheme, you need to understand a few terms. These are explained below.

Expected Week of Confinement (EWC)

This is the week in which the baby is due. Weeks for SMP purposes commence on a Sunday and finish on a Saturday. The expected week of confinement is a key date because all other dates are calculated by working ***backwards*** from the EWC. Look at the example on page 166. In this case, we have assumed that the baby will be born sometime between 7 December and 13 December. We will see how all other times and conditions work backwards from this date.

The employer needs medical evidence of the expected date of birth from a doctor or midwife. Doctors have a special form to notify employers of the expected date of birth. This is form MATB1 (see example on page 170). If the doctor doesn't have a form to hand, he/she can use any other form of written notification.

Qualifying Week (QW)

This week is 15 weeks prior to the week of confinement. It is significant because the employee must have been employed during the qualifying week. 'Employed' by the way includes being on holiday or off sick. In our example, the qualifying week falls between Sunday, 24 August and Saturday, 30 August.

Period of Continuous Employment

This is the period of 26 weeks ending in the Qualifying Week. In our example, the latest start date for the period of continuous employment is 15 March 1997. The employee must have been continuously employed during this period to qualify for SMP. The word 'continuous' needs some clarification. Continuous doesn't mean *every* working day during that period. Part timers qualify even though they only work for as little as half a day a week.

The Statutory Maternity Pay Calendar

1997

	January	February	March
Sunday	5 12 19 26	2 9 16 23	2 9 16 23 30
Monday	6 13 20 27	3 10 17 24	3 10 17 24 31
Tuesday	7 14 21 28	4 11 18 25	4 11 18 25
Wednesday	1 8 15 22 29	5 12 19 26	5 12 19 26
Thursday	2 9 16 23 30	6 13 20 27	6 13 20 27
Friday	3 10 17 24 31	7 14 21 28	7 14 21 28
Saturday	4 11 18 25	1 8 15 22 29	1 8 15 22 29

	April	May	June
Sunday	6 13 20 27	4 11 18 25	1 8 15 22 29
Monday	7 14 21 28	5 12 19 26	2 9 16 23 30
Tuesday	1 8 15 22 29	6 13 20 27	3 10 17 24
Wednesday	2 9 16 23 30	7 14 21 28	4 11 18 25
Thursday	3 10 17 24	1 8 15 22 29	5 12 19 26
Friday	4 11 18 25	2 9 16 23 30	6 13 20 27
Saturday	5 12 19 26	3 10 17 24 31	7 14 21 28

	July	August	September
Sunday	6 13 20 27	3 10 17 24 31	7 14 21 28
Monday	7 14 21 28	4 11 18 25	1 8 15 22 29
Tuesday	1 8 15 22 29	5 12 19 26	2 9 16 23 30
Wednesday	2 9 16 23 30	6 13 20 27	3 10 17 24
Thursday	3 10 17 24 31	7 14 21 28	4 11 18 25
Friday	4 11 18 25	1 8 15 22 29	5 12 19 26
Saturday	5 12 19 26	2 9 16 23 30	6 13 20 27

	October	November	December
Sunday	5 12 19 26	2 9 16 23 30	7 14 21 28
Monday	6 13 20 27	3 10 17 24	1 8 15 22 29
Tuesday	7 14 21 28	4 11 18 25	2 9 16 23 30
Wednesday	1 8 15 22 29	5 12 19 26	3 10 17 24 31
Thursday	2 9 16 23 30	6 13 20 27	4 11 18 25
Friday	3 10 17 24 31	7 14 21 28	5 12 19 26
Saturday	4 11 18 25	1 8 15 22 29	6 13 20 27

26 week 'period of continuous employment'. Employee must have been employed during this period to qualify for SMP.

Pregnancy Week - 1 weeks before baby i due. Employee mus still be pregnant (o have had baby) by thi week to qualify fo SMP.

Expected Week of Confinement (EWC) - week in which baby is expected to be born.

Maternity Pay Period (MPP) - a period of 18 weeks during which SMP is payable.

- Earliest start time is 11 weeks before baby is due
- Latest start time for MPP is Sunday following date of birth.

Qualifying Week (QW) - 15 weeks before the week of confinement. Employee must have been employed in this week.

The period of continuous employment is not broken if the employer lays someone off because of lack of work. So long as the employee is *available* for work then this still qualifies as 'employed' for SMP purposes. Pages 11-17 of the Statutory Maternity Pay Manual give a list of possible interpretations of 'continuous'.

Eleventh Week

The employee must still be pregnant 11 weeks before the baby is due (or have already had the baby) to qualify for SMP. In our example, the eleventh week is between Sunday, 21 September and Saturday, 27 September.

Maternity Pay Period

This is a period of 18 weeks during which an employee is entitled to maternity pay. The first six weeks are payable at 90% of average earnings subject to a minimum payment of £55.70 per week. The remaining 12 weeks are payable at £55.70.

The earliest start time for the maternity pay period is 11 weeks before the baby is due. The latest start time is the Sunday following the baby's birth.

The employee must give the employer three week's notice of commencement of leave. Provided that the employee meets all other conditions shown above then the employer must pay her SMP. Note that the employee is still entitled to be paid even if she doesn't intend to return to work after the baby is born. Other women entitled to SMP include agency workers, part time workers and married women/widows paying reduced rate NI contributions (provided they satisfy the same qualifying conditions as everyone else).

Using SMP Tables

Fortunately, you don't need to work the dates out on a calendar as we did in our example on page 166. The dates have been worked out in the Statutory Maternity Pay Tables CA35/36 from April 1997, see example on page 195. If you know the expected date of birth, you can determine the expected week of confinement in column 1. Once you know the expected week of confinement, you can read off all the other significant dates for calculating eligibility to SMP from columns 2, 3, 4 and 5.

Column 3 — Tells the employer the latest date by which employment must have commenced to enable SMP to be payable.

Column 4	Tells the employer the date on which the employee must still be pregnant for SMP to be due, *and*
Column 5	Tells the employer the last date for commencement of SMP payments if the employee has stopped work.

Non Eligibility for SMP

To be eligible to receive SMP, your employee must satisfy the conditions on page 163. Employees could debar themselves from SMP if:

- They are not in the European Economic Area during the first week of their maternity pay period.

- They are in legal custody during the first week of their maternity pay period.

If you decide that an employee is not entitled to SMP for any reason, you should complete form SMP1 (see page 172) and return any maternity certificate you have been given (keep a photocopy of the maternity certificate for your records). Form SMP1 explains why you cannot pay SMP to your employee. Be aware that the employee can refer your refusal to the local Social Security Office for possible appeal.

If your employee is not eligible for SMP, she may be entitled to claim Maternity Allowance from the DSS. She will need to check whether she is eligible to claim. At the time of writing these notes, Maternity Allowance was worth £55.70 for 18 weeks.

Example

Wendie is expecting a baby, she has average weekly earnings of £145 per week. She has been employed continuously by Mainbrew for five years. Wendie produces a certificate (MATB1) confirming the baby is expected on 17 March 1998.

We must establish:

- the expected week of confinement (EWC)
- the qualifying week (QW) for SMP purposes.

Contd overleaf

Example (Contd)

Refer to the table on page 195 which is an extract from DSS Table CA35/36. We can see from the table that, if the baby is due on 17 March 1998, the expected week of confinement starts on 15 March 1998 in Column 1. We can then read across to Column 2 which tells us that the qualifying week for SMP purposes commences on 30 November 1997.

Wendie would, therefore, be entitled to SMP of:

Higher Rate: £145 x 90% = £130.50 per week for six weeks, and
Lower Rate: £55.70 per week for up to twelve weeks.

Forms, Records and Procedures

Because SMP is a state regulated scheme, you need to keep records which will satisfy the Contributions Agency Inspector should he or she decide to visit you. Fortunately, the Contributions Agency provide you with forms which make this process easy. Here are the records you need to keep.

Employee not eligible for SMP

If you decide that you cannot pay your employee for any reason, be sure to give her a form SMP1 (see page 172). This form clearly states the reason for your refusal. The employee is, of course, free to disagree with you and could take the form to her local Social Security office for advice. The form explains how employees who are unable to get SMP can apply for maternity allowance instead.

Employee eligible for SMP

We suggest you use the checklist on form SMP3 to establish your employee's eligibility to SMP. The form is free and you are unlikely to be criticised for using a form of the DSS's own choosing. The centre pages give you a checklist of all the conditions which must be met before you can pay SMP. The back page gives you a list of all the records which you must keep. Once again, DSS can help by providing a further form SMP2 which contains boxes into which you can enter all the information needed to satisfy the inspector. See example of form SMP2 on page 174. Don't forget to keep a copy of the medical evidence (eg form MATB1) with the employee's form SMP2. Keep all records for at least three years after the end of the tax year to which they relate.

Form MATB1

Maternity Certificate

MAT B1

Please fill in this form in ink

Name of patient

TO THE PATIENT
Please read the note on the back of this form ►

PART A

Fill in this part if you are giving the certificate ***before*** *the confinement*

Do not fill in this form more than 14 weeks before the week when the baby is expected.

I certify that I examined you on the date given below. In my opinion you can expect to have your baby in the week that includes ....../......./......

We use ***week*** *to mean the 7 days starting on a Sunday and ending on a Saturday.*

Date of examination ....../......./......

Date of signing ....../....../......

Signature

PART B

Fill in this part if you are giving the certificate ***after*** *the confinement*

I certify that I attended you in connection with the birth which took place on ..../........./......... when you were delivered of a child [ ] children

In my opinion your baby was expected in the week that includes ..../......../.......

Registered midwives
Please give your UKCC PIN here

Doctors
Please stamp your name and address here if the form had not been stamped by the Family Practitioner Committee.

Payroll Records

Don't forget that SMP is subject to all the normal PAYE and NI deductions. This means that you need to record the pay and deductions on form P11. The year end returns form P14 still shows spaces for you to enter the annual SSP and SMP paid to an employee. However, the Employer's Annual Return forms P35 issued after January 1997 do not show columns for reporting SSP and SMP.

Need to Know More?

The following leaflets will be useful:

- Employer's Quick Guide to Pay As You Earn and National Insurance Contributions CWG1 April 1997, Card No 17

- Statutory Maternity Pay Manual CA29 from April 1997

- Statutory Sick Pay and Statutory Maternity Pay Tables CA35/36 from April 1997

You can also get help via the Employers' helpline 0345-143-143.

Pregnant Women and the Law

There is a great deal of employment legislation designed to protect the employment rights of pregnant women. In this booklet, we have only looked at Statutory Maternity Pay (SMP). There is additional legislation covering:

- Time off for antenatal care
- Protection against unfair dismissal on maternity related grounds
- Maternity leave and maternity absence
- Maternity benefit
- Health and safety.

For guidance on these rights, we suggest an excellent Department of Trade and Industry/ Social Security booklet called 'Maternity Rights - PL958, obtainable free from Cambertown Ltd, Unit 8 Commercial Road, Gowthorpe Industrial Estate, Gowthorpe, Rotherham, SG3 9BL - telephone 01709-888688.

Front of Form SMP1

SMP 1

Statutory Maternity Pay (SMP)

Your Surname

Other names

Address

Postcode

National Insurance (NI) number

Works or clock number

Why I cannot pay you SMP

I have ticked the box which applies to you

☐ I cannot pay you SMP
I have ticked one of the boxes on the next page of this letter to tell you why.

☐ I cannot pay you any more SMP after the week which ends on Saturday / / . You are entitled to weeks SMP from me until then.
I have ticked one of the boxes on the next page of this letter to tell you why I cannot carry on paying you after this date.

What to do if you disagree

If you disagree with this decision, please get in touch with me. My name, address and phone number are at the bottom of this page. If you still disagree, you can ask your social security office for advice. You can find their phone number and address on the advert in the business numbers section of the phone book. Look under **Benefits Agency**. You may be able to ask for an adjudication officer's decision. You can get leaflet **NI 17A** *A guide to Maternity Benefits* from your social security office for more information on this.

Maternity Allowance

You may be able to get Maternity Allowance from your social security office. Ask your ante-natal clinic or social security office for a *Maternity Allowance claim pack.*

How to claim Maternity Allowance

Fill in the claim form **MA1** which is in the pack and send it to your social security office with your *Maternity Certificte* **Mat B1** and this letter. If you gave me your **Mat B1**, I have sent it back to you with this letter. If you want to ask me anything about this letter, please get in touch with me.

Employer's signature

Employer's name and address

Postcode

Phone number

Date / /

Front of Form SMP3

SMP — Statutory Maternity Pay — Form SMP3

Checklist and worksheet

This form is a checklist and worksheet to guide you through the steps you must take to pay, record and get back Statutory Maternity Pay (SMP).

What to do

Use the checklist as a worksheet by filling in the answer spaces as you go.

You will also need:

- form SMP2 or your own SMP record form
- SSP/SMP Tables, CA35/36
- Employer's Quick Guide to Pay As You Earn and National Insurance contributions, CWG1
- SMP Manual, CA29

Employee's full name

Employee's National Insurance Number — Letters / Numbers / Letter

Evidence of pregnancy

1 You must have medical evidence of the date your employee's baby is due. This will normally be a maternity certificate, form MATB1. This certificate is issued to your employee by her doctor or midwife not earlier than 14 weeks before the baby is due. You must not pay SMP until you get medical evidence. See paragraph 16 of CA29.

Can I pay Statutory Maternity Pay?

2 To work out the Expected Week of Confinement (EWC) find out the:
- date your employee's baby is due by checking her form MATB1 **and**
- week the baby is due from column 1 on the SMP tables, CA35/36

When does the EWC start? Day / Month / Year: /   /

3 To find out the Qualifying Week (QW):
- count back 15 weeks from the beginning of the EWC **or**
- look up the date in column 2 on the SMP tables, CA35/36

When does the QW start? Day / Month / Year: /   /

4 Check she will be employed by you in the QW. Please note, she still counts as 'employed by you' if she had her baby prematurely before the QW, but would have still been 'employed by you' if she hadn't.

Is she/can she be treated as employed in the QW?

Yes ☐ Go to step **5**

No ☐ You **cannot** pay SMP. Give her form SMP1 and note this on your own SMP record.

Please turn over ▶

Front of Form SMP2

SMP Statutory Maternity Pay Record Sheet

Employee's name ________ Tax year(s) ___ / ___

National Insurance number ________ ___ / ___

Your Statutory Maternity Pay records
You can use this form for all your Statutory Maternity Pay (SMP) records. You do not have to keep your records on this form. You can keep your records in any way that you find most helpful to you. Or you may want to keep extra records not covered by this form. But you must keep your SMP records for three years after the end of the tax year they are for.

Please look at the quick guide to SMP CA27 (NI268). This explains how and when you must pay SMP and what records you must keep. The SMP tables that we sent you at the start of the tax year will also help you with your records. Our checklist form SMP 3 could also help you.

How to use this form
The record sheet is in two parts. Use **Part A** when your employee tells you the date she wants to start her maternity absence and as her maternity absence begins. Use **Part B** when she might be able to get SMP.

Help and advice
If you need help with this form or with the SMP scheme please get in touch with your local contribution agency office, the telephone number and address are in the telephone book under **"Contributions Agency"** or **"Social Security, Department of"**. You can also get extra copies of the quick guide to SMP CA27 (NI268) or any of the SMP forms through them. Alternatively you can contact the Social Security Advice line for Employers (SSALE) on 0800 393 539.

Part A Records of notification of maternity absence

1. **What date does she intend to start her maternity absence?** ___ / ___ / ___
   Enter the date as soon as you know it.

2. **What date did she tell you about her maternity absence?** ___ / ___ / ___
   You may also find it useful to have a record of this date if she appeals about your decision

3. **What date did she start her maternity absence?** ___ / ___ / ___
   Fill in this date if it is different from the date at question 1.

4. **What is her expected week of confinement (EWC)?** ___ / ___ / ___
   Her doctor or midwife will give her medical evidence of this date. The evidence will be the Maternity Certificate form **Mat B1** or other acceptable evidence. Keep this or a copy of it with your records for three years.

5. **What date was her actual week of confinement?** ___ / ___ / ___
   Fill in this date if her baby was born early and this changed the date you could start to pay her SMP.

6. **What date is her qualifying week (QW)?** ___ / ___ / ___
   This week is 15 weeks before the EWC. You can find it from column 2 of your SMP tables.

7. **Have you excluded her from SMP?** **No** ☐ **Yes** ☐ **From what date?** ___ / ___ / ___

8. **Did you give her an exclusion form SMP1?** **No** ☐ **Yes** ☐
   You can get these forms through your local Social Security office.

SMP 2

Please turn over for Part B →

Back of Form SMP2

Part B Record of Maternity Pay Period

Employee's name ______ Tax year(s) ___ / ___

National Insurance number ☐☐ ☐☐ ☐☐ ☐☐ ☐ ___ / ___

The Maternity Pay Period
The Maternity Pay Period (MPP) is the time when you could pay SMP.
It cannot be longer than 18 weeks.

- The quick guide to SMP CA27 (NI268) will tell you more about this.

You must keep a record of this period even if your employee cannot get SMP for any week or does not come back to work when her baby is born. But if you exclude her completely from SMP at the beginning of the MPP you only need to fill in the first week of the record.

	MPP weeks always begin on a Sunday. Note the date of each week until the MPP ends.	Show number of tax week MPP week is in.	Tick one box for each week W = Worked P = paid SMP E = excluded from SMP. Put reasons in **Notes** column.			Show how much SMP paid in each week.	This will help you to calculate how much SMP you can get back.	Note here any exclusion reasons.
	Sunday of MMP week	**Tax week No**	**Worked**	**Paid**	**Excluded**	**Amount of SMP paid**	**Running total of SMP**	**Notes**
1	/ /		W ☐	P ☐	E ☐	£	£	
2	/ /		W ☐	P ☐	E ☐	£	£	
3	/ /		W ☐	P ☐	E ☐	£	£	
4	/ /		W ☐	P ☐	E ☐	£	£	
5	/ /		W ☐	P ☐	E ☐	£	£	
6	/ /		W ☐	P ☐	E ☐	£	£	
7	/ /		W ☐	P ☐	E ☐	£	£	
8	/ /		W ☐	P ☐	E ☐	£	£	
9	/ /		W ☐	P ☐	E ☐	£	£	
10	/ /		W ☐	P ☐	E ☐	£	£	
11	/ /		W ☐	P ☐	E ☐	£	£	
12	/ /		W ☐	P ☐	E ☐	£	£	
13	/ /		W ☐	P ☐	E ☐	£	£	
14	/ /		W ☐	P ☐	E ☐	£	£	
15	/ /		W ☐	P ☐	E ☐	£	£	
16	/ /		W ☐	P ☐	E ☐	£	£	
17	/ /		W ☐	P ☐	E ☐	£	£	
18	/ /		W ☐	P ☐	E ☐	£	£	

Printed in the UK for BAPSS by CPM Ltd T3550/5-94/

Appendix 1

Tax Publications Guide

The most commonly used manuals are posted to employers around February or March each year. This collection of manuals is called the Employer's Annual Pack.

Here is a list of the forms and manuals in the 1997 Annual Pack:

CWG3	Annual Pack Orderline details
P9X(1997)	November 1996 Budget Proposals Self Assessment Newsletter
CWG1	Employer's Quick Guide to Pay As You Earn and National Insurance Contributions April 1997
CWG2	Employer's Further Guide to PAYE and NICs (1997)
CA38	National Insurance Not Contracted Out Contributions Tables from April 1997
CA35/36	Statutory Sick Pay and Statutory Maternity Pay Tables from April 1997
Tables LR+B-D	Taxable Pay Tables April 1997 issue
480(1997)	Expenses and Benefits - A Tax Guide

The following pages show a selection of useful manuals, tables, forms and leaflets which are free and may be of use to you. Most are either available from the Employers' Orderline 0345-646-646 or your local tax office.

Inland Revenue/Contributions Agency Manuals and Tables

P9X(1997)	November 1996 Budget Proposals - What you must do
Tables LR+B-D	Taxable Pay Tables April 1997 issue (BMSD 12/96)
CA44	National Insurance for Company Directors
CWG1	Employer's Quick Guide to Pay As You Earn and National Insurance Contributions April 1997
CWG2	Employer's Further Guide to PAYE and NICs (1997)
CA35/36	Statutory Sick Pay and Statutory Maternity Pay Tables from April 1997
CA38	National Insurance Not Contracted Out Contributions Tables from April 1997
480 (1997)	Expenses and Benefits - A Tax Guide
P11(D) Guide 1997	P11D Guide 1996-1997
CA29	Employer's Manual on Statutory Maternity Pay
CA30	Employer's Manual on Statutory Sick Pay
CA33	Employer's Manual on Class 1A National Insurance Contributions on Cars and Fuel (also supplement)
P11(Int)	Details of official rates of interest in 1996-1997

Inland Revenue/Contributions Agency Forms

P9D(1997)	Return of Expenses payments and income from which tax cannot be deducted 1996-1997
P11(D)(1997)	Return of Expenses and Benefits - Employer's Declaration 1996-1997 BMSD11/96
FPCS2(1997)	Fixed Profit Car Scheme - Information for Employees' Tax Returns
P11DWS	P11D Working Sheets (five off)
CA6855	National Insurance Number Trace
P11(1997)	Deductions Working Sheets
P32	Employer's Payment Record
P30B	Payslips for sending with payments to the Accounts Office
P30BC	Payslip booklet containing payslips

P31	For use by a new employer who wishes to pay quarterly
P34	For ordering fresh supplies of forms from your tax office
P35	Employer's annual return
P38	Employer's supplementary return for employees who were not entered onP38Aform P35
P38S	For use by students to claim special treatment when employed during holidays
P45	For use where an employee leaves a job and when an employee starts a job
P46	For use when a new employee does not produce a P45
P46(Car)	Advance details of car/fuel provided for employee
P60	Certificate of employee's pay and tax deducted. This can be either a separate form or the third part of form P14

Inland Revenue Leaflets and Guides

Leaflet No	Pubn Date	Title
IR (Insert)	12/96	Proposed allowances and rates of tax for 1997-98
IR34	1/96	PAYE. Pay As You Earn
IR43	7/92	Income tax and strikes
IR53	4/95	Thinking of taking someone on? PAYE for employers
IR56/NI39	5/95	Employed or self-employed? A guide for tax and National Insurance
IR60	11/95	Income tax and students
IR65	11/93	Giving to charity. How individuals can get tax relief
IR69	2/96	Expenses payments:forms P11D. How to save yourself work
IR71	5/93	PAYE inspections. Employers' and contractors' records
IR76	1991	Personal Pension Schemes. Guidance notes
IR78	12/91	Personal pensions. A guide for tax
IR90	8/94	Tax allowances and reliefs
IR95	6/96	Approved profit sharing schemes. An outline for employees

IR97	6/96	Approved SAYE share option schemes. An outline for employees
IR98	6/96	Approved SAYE share option schemes. Explanatory notes
IR109	5/93	PAYE inspections and negotiations. Employers' and contractors' records. How settlements are negotiated
IR119	5/93	Tax relief for vocational training
IR120	5/94	You and the Inland Revenue. Tax, Collection and Accounts Offices
IR120	7/95	You and the Pensions Schemes Office
IR121	5/95	Income tax and pensioners
IR125	3/96	Using your own car for work
IR129	6/95	Occupational pension schemes. An introduction
IR132	10/93	Taxation of company cars from 6 April 1994. Employers' guide
IR133	11/93	Income tax and company cars from 6 April 1994. A guide for employees
IR134	6/94	Income tax and relocation packages
IR136	3/94	Income tax and company vans. A guide for employees and employers
IR148/CA69	10/95	Are your workers employed or self-employed? A guide for tax and National Insurance for contractors in the construction industry
IR155	11/96	PAYE settlement agreements
SAT3	8/95	Self Assessment. What it will mean for employers
480	4/96	Expenses and benefits. A guide for tax
CWG2	11/96	Employer's further guide to Pay As You Earn and NICs
COP2	5/95	Investigations
COP3	2/93	Inspections of employers' and contractors' records

Sample Tax Tables

Month 1 TABLE A - PAY ADJUSTMENT

Apr 6 to May 5

Code	Total pay adjustment to date	Code	Total pay adjustment to date	Code	Total pay adjustment to date	Code	Total pay adjustment to date	Code	Total pay adjustment to date	Code	Total pay adjustment to date	Code	Total pay adjustment to date	Code	Total pay adjustment to date	Code	Total pay adjustment to date
	£		£		£		£		£		£		£		£		£
0	NIL																
1	1.59	61	51.59	121	101.59	181	151.59	241	201.59	301	251.59	351	293.25	401	334.92	451	376.59
2	2.42	62	52.42	122	102.42	182	152.42	242	202.42	302	252.42	352	294.09	402	335.75	452	377.42
3	3.25	63	53.25	123	103.25	183	153.25	243	203.25	303	253.25	353	294.92	403	336.59	453	378.25
4	4.09	64	54.09	124	104.09	184	154.09	244	204.09	304	254.09	354	295.75	404	337.42	454	379.09
5	4.92	65	54.92	125	104.92	185	154.92	245	204.92	305	254.92	355	296.59	405	338.25	455	379.92
6	5.75	66	55.75	126	105.75	186	155.75	246	205.75	306	255.75	356	297.42	406	339.09	456	380.75
7	6.59	67	56.59	127	106.59	187	156.59	247	206.59	307	256.59	357	298.25	407	339.92	457	381.59
8	7.42	68	57.42	128	107.42	188	157.42	248	207.42	308	257.42	358	299.09	408	340.75	458	382.42
9	8.25	69	58.25	129	108.25	189	158.25	249	208.25	309	258.25	359	299.92	409	341.59	459	383.25
10	9.09	70	59.09	130	109.09	190	159.09	250	209.09	310	259.09	360	300.75	410	342.42	460	384.09
11	9.92	71	59.92	131	109.92	191	159.92	251	209.92	311	259.92	361	301.59	411	343.25	461	384.92
12	10.75	72	60.75	132	110.75	192	160.75	252	210.75	312	260.75	362	302.42	412	344.09	462	385.75
13	11.59	73	61.59	133	111.59	193	161.59	253	211.59	313	261.59	363	303.25	413	344.92	463	386.59
14	12.42	74	62.42	134	112.42	194	162.42	254	212.42	314	262.42	364	304.09	414	345.75	464	387.42
15	13.25	75	63.25	135	113.25	195	163.25	255	213.25	315	263.25	365	304.92	415	346.59	465	388.25
16	14.09	76	64.09	136	114.09	196	164.09	256	214.09	316	264.09	366	305.75	416	347.42	466	389.09
17	14.92	77	64.92	137	114.92	197	164.92	257	214.92	317	264.92	367	306.59	417	348.25	467	389.92
18	15.75	78	65.75	138	115.75	198	165.75	258	215.75	318	265.75	368	307.42	418	349.09	468	390.75
19	16.59	79	66.59	139	116.59	199	166.59	259	216.59	319	266.59	369	308.25	419	349.92	469	391.59
20	17.42	80	67.42	140	117.42	200	167.42	260	217.42	320	267.42	370	309.09	420	350.75	470	392.42
21	18.25	81	68.25	141	118.25	201	168.25	261	218.25	321	268.25	371	309.92	421	351.59	471	393.25
22	19.09	82	69.09	142	119.09	202	169.09	262	219.09	322	269.09	372	310.75	422	352.42	472	394.09
23	19.92	83	69.92	143	119.92	203	169.92	263	219.92	323	269.92	373	311.59	423	353.25	473	394.92
24	20.75	84	70.75	144	120.75	204	170.75	264	220.75	324	270.75	374	312.42	424	354.09	474	395.75
25	21.59	85	71.59	145	121.59	205	171.59	265	221.59	325	271.59	375	313.25	425	354.92	475	396.59
26	22.42	86	72.42	146	122.42	206	172.42	266	222.42	326	272.42	376	314.09	426	355.75	476	397.42
27	23.25	87	73.25	147	123.25	207	173.25	267	223.25	327	273.25	377	314.92	427	356.59	477	398.25
28	24.09	88	74.09	148	124.09	208	174.09	268	224.09	328	274.09	378	315.75	428	357.42	478	399.09
29	24.92	89	74.92	149	124.92	209	174.92	269	224.92	329	274.92	379	316.59	429	358.25	479	399.92
30	25.75	90	75.75	150	125.75	210	175.75	270	225.75	330	275.75	380	317.42	430	359.09	480	400.75
31	26.59	91	76.59	151	126.59	211	176.59	271	226.59	331	276.59	381	318.25	431	359.92	481	401.59
32	27.42	92	77.42	152	127.42	212	177.42	272	227.42	332	277.42	382	319.09	432	360.75	482	402.42
33	28.25	93	78.25	153	128.25	213	178.25	273	228.25	333	278.25	383	319.92	433	361.59	483	403.25
34	29.09	94	79.09	154	129.09	214	179.09	274	229.09	334	279.09	384	320.75	434	362.42	484	404.09
35	29.92	95	79.92	155	129.92	215	179.92	275	229.92	335	279.92	385	321.59	435	363.25	485	404.92
36	30.75	96	80.75	156	130.75	216	180.75	276	230.75	336	280.75	386	322.42	436	364.09	486	405.75
37	31.59	97	81.59	157	131.59	217	181.59	277	231.59	337	281.59	387	323.25	437	364.92	487	406.59
38	32.42	98	82.42	158	132.42	218	182.42	278	232.42	338	282.42	388	324.09	438	365.75	488	407.42
39	33.25	99	83.25	159	133.25	219	183.25	279	233.25	339	283.25	389	324.92	439	366.59	499	408.25
40	34.09	100	84.09	160	134.09	220	184.09	280	234.09	340	284.09	390	325.75	440	367.42	490	409.09
41	34.92	101	84.92	161	134.92	221	184.92	281	234.92	341	284.92	391	326.59	441	368.25	491	409.92
42	35.75	102	85.75	162	135.75	222	185.75	282	235.75	342	285.75	392	327.42	442	369.09	492	410.75
43	36.59	103	86.59	163	136.59	223	186.59	283	236.59	343	286.59	393	328.25	443	369.92	493	411.59
44	37.42	104	87.42	164	137.42	224	187.42	284	237.42	344	287.42	394	329.09	444	370.75	494	412.42
45	38.25	105	88.25	165	138.25	225	188.25	285	238.25	345	288.25	395	329.92	445	371.59	495	413.25
46	39.09	106	89.09	166	139.09	226	189.09	286	239.09	346	289.09	396	330.75	446	372.42	496	414.09
47	39.92	107	89.92	167	139.92	227	189.92	287	239.92	347	289.92	397	331.59	447	373.25	497	414.92
48	40.75	108	90.75	168	140.75	228	190.75	288	240.75	348	290.75	398	332.42	448	374.09	498	415.75
49	41.59	109	91.59	169	141.59	229	191.59	289	241.59	349	291.59	399	333.25	449	374.92	499	416.59
50	42.42	110	92.42	170	142.42	230	192.42	290	242.42	350	292.42	400	334.09	450	375.75	500	417.42
51	43.25	111	93.25	171	143.25	231	193.25	291	243.25								
52	44.09	112	94.09	172	144.09	232	194.09	292	244.09								
53	44.92	113	94.92	173	144.92	233	194.92	293	244.92								
54	45.75	114	95.75	174	145.75	234	195.75	294	245.75								
55	46.59	115	96.59	175	146.59	235	196.59	295	246.59								
56	47.42	116	97.42	176	147.42	236	197.42	296	247.42								
57	48.25	117	98.25	177	148.25	237	198.25	297	248.25								
58	49.09	118	99.09	178	149.09	238	199.09	298	249.09								
59	49.92	119	99.92	179	149.92	239	199.92	299	249.92								
60	50.75	120	100.75	180	150.75	240	200.75	300	250.75								

Pay adjustment where code exceeds 500

1. Where the code is in the range **501** to **1000** inclusive proceed as follows:
   a. Subtract **500** from the code and use the balance of the code to obtain a pay adjustment figure from the table above.
   b. Add this pay adjustment figure to the figure given in the box alongside to obtain the figure of total adjustment to date * **416.67**
2. Where the code **exceeds 1000** follow the instructions on **page 2**.

TABLE A - PAY ADJUSTMENT Month 2

May 6 to June 5

Code	Total pay adjustment to date	Code	Total pay adjustment to date	Code	Total pay adjustment to date	Code	Total pay adjustment to date	Code	Total pay adjustment to date	Code	Total pay adjustment to date	Code	Total pay adjustment to date	Code	Total pay adjustment to date	Code	Total pay adjustment to date
	£		£		£		£		£		£		£		£		£
0	NIL																
1	3.18	61	103.18	121	203.18	181	303.18	241	403.18	301	503.18	351	586.50	401	669.84	451	753.18
2	4.84	62	104.84	122	204.84	182	304.84	242	404.84	302	504.84	352	588.18	402	671.50	452	754.84
3	6.50	63	106.50	123	206.50	183	306.50	243	406.50	303	506.50	353	589.84	403	673.18	453	756.50
4	8.18	64	108.18	124	208.18	184	308.18	244	408.18	304	508.18	354	591.50	404	674.84	454	758.18
5	9.84	65	109.84	125	209.84	185	309.84	245	409.84	305	509.84	355	593.18	405	676.50	455	759.84
6	11.50	66	111.50	126	211.50	186	311.50	246	411.50	306	511.50	356	594.84	406	678.18	456	761.50
7	13.18	67	113.18	127	213.18	187	313.18	247	413.18	307	513.18	357	596.50	407	679.84	457	763.18
8	14.84	68	114.84	128	214.84	188	314.84	248	414.84	308	514.84	358	598.18	408	681.50	458	764.84
9	16.50	69	116.50	129	216.50	189	316.50	249	416.50	309	516.50	359	599.84	409	683.18	459	766.50
10	18.18	70	118.18	130	218.18	190	318.18	250	418.18	310	518.18	360	601.50	410	684.84	460	768.18
11	19.84	71	119.84	131	219.84	191	319.84	251	419.84	311	519.84	361	603.18	411	686.50	461	769.84
12	21.50	72	121.50	132	221.50	192	321.50	252	421.50	312	521.50	362	604.84	412	688.18	462	771.50
13	23.18	73	123.18	133	223.18	193	323.18	253	423.18	313	523.18	363	606.50	413	689.84	463	773.18
14	24.84	74	124.84	134	224.84	194	324.84	254	424.84	314	524.84	364	608.18	414	691.50	464	774.84
15	26.50	75	126.50	135	226.50	195	326.50	255	426.50	315	526.50	365	609.84	415	693.18	465	776.50
16	28.18	76	128.18	136	228.18	196	328.18	256	428.18	316	528.18	366	611.50	416	694.84	466	778.18
17	29.84	77	129.84	137	229.84	197	329.84	257	429.84	317	529.84	367	613.18	417	696.50	467	779.84
18	31.50	78	131.50	138	231.50	198	331.50	258	431.50	318	531.50	368	614.84	418	698.18	468	781.50
19	33.18	79	133.18	139	233.18	199	333.18	259	433.18	319	533.18	369	616.50	419	699.84	469	783.18
20	34.84	80	134.84	140	234.84	200	334.84	260	434.84	320	534.84	370	618.18	420	701.50	470	784.84
21	36.50	81	136.50	141	236.50	201	336.50	261	436.50	321	536.50	371	619.84	421	703.18	471	786.50
22	38.18	82	138.18	142	238.18	202	338.18	262	438.18	322	538.18	372	621.50	422	704.84	472	788.18
23	39.84	83	139.84	143	239.84	203	339.84	263	439.84	323	539.84	373	623.18	423	706.50	473	789.84
24	41.50	84	141.50	144	241.50	204	341.50	264	441.50	324	541.50	374	624.84	424	708.18	474	791.50
25	43.18	85	143.18	145	243.18	205	343.18	265	443.18	325	543.18	375	626.50	425	709.84	475	793.18
26	44.84	86	144.84	146	244.84	206	344.84	266	444.84	326	544.84	376	628.18	426	711.50	476	794.84
27	46.50	87	146.50	147	246.50	207	346.50	267	446.50	327	546.50	377	629.84	427	713.18	477	796.50
28	48.18	88	148.18	148	248.18	208	348.18	268	448.18	328	548.18	378	631.50	428	714.84	478	798.18
29	49.84	89	149.84	149	249.84	209	349.84	269	449.84	329	549.84	379	633.18	429	716.50	479	799.84
30	51.50	90	151.50	150	251.50	210	351.50	270	451.50	330	551.50	380	634.84	430	718.18	480	801.50
31	53.18	91	153.18	151	253.18	211	353.18	271	453.18	331	553.18	381	636.50	431	719.84	481	803.18
32	54.84	92	154.84	152	254.84	212	354.84	272	454.84	332	554.84	382	638.18	432	721.50	482	804.84
33	56.50	93	156.50	153	256.50	213	356.50	273	456.50	333	556.50	383	639.84	433	723.18	483	806.50
34	58.18	94	158.18	154	258.18	214	358.18	274	458.18	334	558.18	384	641.50	434	724.84	484	808.18
35	59.84	95	159.84	155	259.84	215	359.84	275	459.84	335	559.84	385	643.18	435	726.50	485	809.84
36	61.50	96	161.50	156	261.50	216	361.50	276	461.50	336	561.50	386	644.84	436	728.18	486	811.50
37	63.18	97	163.18	157	263.18	217	363.18	277	463.18	337	563.18	387	646.50	437	729.84	487	813.18
38	64.84	98	164.84	158	264.84	218	364.84	278	464.84	338	564.84	388	648.18	438	731.50	488	814.84
39	66.50	99	166.50	159	266.50	219	366.50	279	466.50	339	566.50	389	649.84	439	733.18	489	816.50
40	68.18	100	168.18	160	268.18	220	368.18	280	468.18	340	568.18	390	651.50	440	734.84	490	818.18
41	69.84	101	169.84	161	269.84	221	369.84	281	469.84	341	569.84	391	653.18	441	736.50	491	819.84
42	71.50	102	171.50	162	271.50	222	371.50	282	471.50	342	571.50	392	654.84	442	738.18	492	821.50
43	73.18	103	173.18	163	273.18	223	373.18	283	473.18	343	573.18	393	656.50	443	739.84	493	823.18
44	74.84	104	174.84	164	274.84	224	374.84	284	474.84	344	574.84	394	658.18	444	741.50	494	824.84
45	76.50	105	176.50	165	276.50	225	376.50	285	476.50	345	576.50	395	659.84	445	743.18	495	826.50
46	78.18	106	178.18	166	278.18	226	378.18	286	478.18	346	578.18	396	661.50	446	744.84	496	828.18
47	79.84	107	179.84	167	279.84	227	379.84	287	479.84	347	579.84	397	663.18	447	746.50	497	829.84
48	81.50	108	181.50	168	281.50	228	381.50	288	481.50	348	581.50	398	664.84	448	748.18	498	831.50
49	83.18	109	183.18	169	283.18	229	383.18	289	483.18	349	583.18	399	666.50	449	749.84	499	833.18
50	84.84	110	184.84	170	284.84	230	384.84	290	484.84	350	584.84	400	668.18	450	751.50	500	834.84
51	86.50	111	186.50	171	286.50	231	386.50	291	486.50								
52	88.18	112	188.18	172	288.18	232	388.18	292	488.18								
53	89.84	113	189.84	173	289.84	233	389.84	293	489.84								
54	91.50	114	191.50	174	291.50	234	391.50	294	491.50								
55	93.18	115	193.18	175	293.18	235	393.18	295	493.18								
56	94.84	116	194.84	176	294.84	236	394.84	296	494.84								
57	96.50	117	196.50	177	296.50	237	396.50	297	496.50								
58	98.18	118	198.18	178	298.18	238	398.18	298	498.18								
59	99.84	119	199.84	179	299.84	239	399.84	299	499.84								
60	101.50	120	201.50	180	301.50	240	401.50	300	501.50								

Pay adjustment where code exceeds 500

1. Where the code is in the range **501** to **1000** inclusive proceed as follows:
   - **a.** Subtract **500** from the code and use the balance of the code to obtain a pay adjustment figure from the table above.
   - **b.** Add this pay adjustment figure to the figure given in the box alongside to obtain the figure of total adjustment to date * **833.34**
2. Where the code **exceeds 1000** follow the instructions on **page 2**.

Pay at Monthly rates

Which tax table to use?

For Code BR use Table B on Page 6
For Code DO use Table D on Pages 10 and 11
For other codes:-

Month No.	1 Use table LR (Page 4) when the *total taxable pay* to date ***does not exceed***	2 Use table B (Pages 6 **&** 7) when the *total taxable pay* to date ***exceeds*** the Column 1 figure ***but does not exceed***	3 Use tables C and D (Pages 9 - 11) when the *total taxable pay* to date ***exceeds***	Month No.
	£	£	£	
1	does not exceed 342	does not exceed 2175	exceeds 2175	1
2	684	4350	4350	2
3	1025	6525	6525	3
4	1367	8700	8700	4
5	1709	10875	10875	5
6	2050	13050	13050	6
7	2392	15225	15225	7
8	2734	17400	17400	8
9	3075	19575	19575	9
10	3417	21750	21750	10
11	3759	23925	23925	11
12	4100	26100	26100	12

Pages 2 and 3 tell you when to use this table

Table LR

(Tax at 20%)

Tax Due on Taxable Pay from £1 to £99

Total TAXABLE PAY to date	Total TAX DUE to date	Total TAXABLE PAY to date	Total TAX DUE to date
£	£	£	£
1	0.20	61	12.20
2	0.40	62	12.40
3	0.60	63	12.60
4	0.80	64	12.80
5	1.00	65	13.00
6	1.20	66	13.20
7	1.40	67	13.40
8	1.60	68	13.60
9	1.80	69	13.80
10	2.00	70	14.00
11	2.20	71	14.20
12	2.40	72	14.40
13	2.60	73	14.60
14	2.80	74	14.80
15	3.00	75	15.00
16	3.20	76	15.20
17	3.40	77	15.40
18	3.60	78	15.60
19	3.80	79	15.80
20	4.00	80	16.00
21	4.20	81	16.20
22	4.40	82	16.40
23	4.60	83	16.60
24	4.80	84	16.80
25	5.00	85	17.00
26	5.20	86	17.20
27	5.40	87	17.40
28	5.60	88	17.60
29	5.80	89	17.80
30	6.00	90	18.00
31	6.20	91	18.20
32	6.40	92	18.40
33	6.60	93	18.60
34	6.80	94	18.80
35	7.00	95	19.00
36	7.20	96	19.20
37	7.40	97	19.40
38	7.60	98	19.60
39	7.80	99	19.80
40	8 00		
41	8.20		
42	8.40		
43	8.60		
44	8.80		
45	9.00		
46	9.20		
47	9.40		
48	9.60		
49	9.80		
50	10.00		
51	10.20		
52	10.40		
53	10.60		
54	10.80		
55	11.00		
56	11.20		
57	11.40		
58	11.60		
59	11.80		
60	12.00		

Tax Due on Taxable Pay from £100 to £4100

Total TAXABLE PAY to date	Total TAX DUE to date
£	£
100	20.00
200	40.00
300	60.00
400	80.00
500	100.00
600	120.00
700	140.00
800	160.00
900	180.00
1000	200.00
1100	220.00
1200	240.00
1300	260.00
1400	280.00
1500	300.00
1600	320.00
1700	340.00
1800	360.00
1900	380.00
2000	400.00
2100	420.00
2200	440.00
2300	460.00
2400	480.00
2500	500.00
2600	520.00
2700	540.00
2800	560.00
2900	580.00
3000	600.00
3100	620.00
3200	640.00
3300	660.00
3400	680.00
3500	700.00
3600	720.00
3700	740.00
3800	760.00
3900	780.00
4000	800.00
4100	820.00

Where the exact amount of taxable pay is not shown, add together the figures for two (or more) entries to make up the amount of taxable pay to the nearest £1 below

Pages 2 and 3 tell you when to use these tables

Table B
(Tax at 23%)

Remember to use the Subtraction Tables on Page 7

Tax Due on Taxable Pay from £1 to £99

Total TAXABLE PAY to dale	Total TAX DUE to date	Total TAXABLE PAY to date	Total TAX DUE to date
£	£	£	£
1	0.23	56	12.88
2	0.46	57	13.11
3	0.69	58	13.34
4	0.92	59	13.57
5	1.15	60	13.80
6	1.38	61	14.03
7	1.61	62	14.26
8	1.84	63	14.49
9	2.07	64	14.72
10	2.30	65	14.95
11	2.53	66	15.18
12	2.76	67	15.41
13	2.99	68	15.64
14	3.22	69	15.87
15	3.45	70	16.10
16	3.68	71	16.33
17	3.91	72	16.56
18	4.14	73	16.79
19	4.37	74	17.02
20	4.60	75	17.25
21	4.83	76	17.48
22	5.06	77	17.71
23	5.29	78	17.94
24	5.52	79	18.17
25	5.75	80	18.40
26	5.98	81	18.63
27	6.21	82	18.86
28	6.44	83	19.09
29	6.67	84	19.32
30	6.90	85	19.55
31	7.13	86	19.78
32	7.36	87	20.01
33	7.59	88	20.24
34	7.82	89	20.47
35	8.05	90	20.70
36	8.28	91	20.93
37	8.51	92	21.16
38	8.74	93	21.39
39	8.97	94	21.62
40	9.20	95	21.85
41	9.43	96	22.08
42	9.66	97	22.31
43	9.89	98	22.54
44	10.12	99	22.77
45	10.35		
46	10.58		
47	10.81		
48	11.04		
49	11.27		
50	11.50		
51	11.73		
52	11.96		
53	12.19		
54	12.42		
55	12.65		

Where the exact amount of taxable pay is not shown, add together the figures for two (or more) entries to make up the amount of taxable pay to the nearest £1 below

Tax Due on Taxable Pay from £100 to £26,000

Total TAXABLE PAY to date	Total TAX DUE to date	Total TAXABLE PAY to date	Total TAX DUE to date	Total TAXABLE PAY to date	Total TAX DUE to date	Total TAXABLE PAY to date	Total TAX DUE to date
£	£	£	£	£	£	£	£
100	23.00	6600	1518.00	13100	3013.00	19600	4508.00
200	46.00	6700	1541.00	13200	3036.00	19700	4531.00
300	69.00	6800	1564.00	13300	3059.00	19800	4554.00
400	92.00	6900	1587.00	13400	3082.00	19900	4577.00
500	115.00	7000	1610.00	13500	3105.00	20000	4600.00
600	138.00	7100	1633.00	13600	3128.00	20100	4623.00
700	161.00	7200	1656.00	13700	3151.00	20200	4646.00
800	184.00	7300	1679.00	13800	3174.00	20300	4669.00
900	207.00	7400	1702.00	13900	3197.00	20400	4692.00
1000	230.00	7500	1725.00	14000	3220.00	20500	4715.00
1100	253.00	7600	1748.00	14100	3243.00	20600	4738.00
1200	276.00	7700	1771.00	14200	3266.00	20700	4761.00
1300	299.00	7800	1794.00	14300	3289.00	20800	4784.00
1400	322.00	7900	1817.00	14400	3312.00	20900	4807.00
1500	345.00	8000	1840.00	14500	3335.00	21000	4830.00
1600	368.00	8100	1863.00	14600	3358.00	21100	4853.00
1700	391.00	8200	1886.00	14700	3381.00	21200	4876.00
1800	414.00	8300	1909.00	14800	3404.00	21300	4899.00
1900	437.00	8400	1932.00	14900	3427.00	21400	4922.00
2000	460.00	8500	1955.00	15000	3450.00	21500	4945.00
2100	483.00	8600	1978.00	15100	3473.00	21600	4968.00
2200	506.00	8700	2001.00	15200	3496.00	21700	4991.00
2300	529.00	8800	2024.00	15300	3519.00	21800	5014.00
2400	552.00	8900	2047.00	15400	3542.00	21900	5037.00
2500	575.00	9000	2070.00	15500	3565.00	22000	5060.00
2600	598.00	9100	2093.00	15600	3588.00	22100	5083.00
2700	621.00	9200	2116.00	15700	3611.00	22200	5106.00
2800	644.00	9300	2139.00	15800	3634.00	22300	5129.00
2900	667.00	9400	2162.00	15900	3657.00	22400	5152.00
3000	690.00	9500	2185.00	16000	3680.00	22500	5175.00
3100	713.00	9600	2208.00	16100	3703.00	22600	5198.00
3200	736.00	9700	2231.00	16200	3726.00	22700	5221.00
3300	759.00	9800	2254.00	16300	3749.00	22800	5244.00
3400	782.00	9900	2277.00	16400	3772.00	22900	5267.00
3500	805.00	10000	2300.00	16500	3795.00	23000	5290.00
3600	828.00	10100	2323.00	16600	3818.00	23100	5313.00
3700	851.00	10200	2346.00	16700	3841.00	23200	5336.00
3800	874.00	10300	2369.00	16800	3864.00	23300	5359.00
3900	897.00	10400	2392.00	16900	3887.00	23400	5382.00
4000	920.00	10500	2415.00	17000	3910.00	23500	5405.00
4100	943.00	10600	2438.00	17100	3933.00	23600	5428.00
4200	966.00	10700	2461.00	17200	3956.00	23700	5451.00
4300	989.00	10800	2484.00	17300	3979.00	23800	5474.00
4400	1012.00	10900	2507.00	17400	4002.00	23900	5497.00
4500	1035.00	11000	2530.00	17500	4025.00	24000	5520.00
4600	1158.00	11100	2553.00	17600	4048.00	24100	5543.00
4700	1081.00	11200	2576.00	17700	4071.00	24200	5566.00
4800	1104.00	11300	2599.00	17800	4094.00	24300	5589.00
4900	1127.00	11400	2622.00	17900	4117.00	24400	5612.00
5000	1150.00	11500	2645.00	18000	4140.00	24500	5635.00
5100	1173.00	11600	2668.00	18100	4163.00	24600	5658.00
5200	1196.00	11700	2691.00	18200	4186.00	24700	5681.00
5300	1219.00	11800	2714.00	18300	4209.00	24800	5704.00
5400	1242.00	11900	2737.00	18400	4232.00	24900	5727.00
5500	1265.00	12000	2760.00	18500	4255.00	25000	5750.00
5600	1288.00	12100	2783.00	18600	4278.00	25100	5773.00
5700	1311.00	12200	2806.00	18700	4301.00	25200	5796.00
5800	1334.00	12300	2829.00	18800	4324.00	25300	5819.00
5900	1357.00	12400	2852.00	18900	4347.00	25400	5842.00
6000	1380.00	12500	2875.00	19000	4370.00	25500	5865.00
6100	1403.00	12600	2898.00	19100	4393.00	25600	5888.00
6200	1426.00	12700	2921.00	19200	4416.00	25700	5911.00
6300	1449.00	12800	2944.00	19300	4439.00	25800	5934.00
6400	1472.00	12900	2967.00	19400	4462.00	25900	5957.00
6500	1495.00	13000	2990.00	19500	4485.00	26000	5980.00

Table B Subtraction Tables

(Lower Rate Relief)

Do not use the subtraction tables for code BR

For all ordinary suffix codes and prefix K codes - When you have used the table on Page 6 to work out the tax at 23% refer to the tables below to give the benefit of the lower rate band. Find the week or month in which the pay day falls (it is the same week or month you have used in Tables A) and **subtract** the amount shown to arrive at the tax due.

There is an example below and further examples on Page 8

Employee paid at Weekly rates

Week No	Amount to subtract £
1	2.37
2	4.74
3	7.10
4	9.47
5	11.83
6	14.20
7	16.56
8	18.93
9	21.29
10	23.66
11	26.02
12	28.39
13	30.75
14	33.12
15	35.49
16	37.85
17	40.22
18	42.58
19	44.95
20	47.31
21	49.68
22	52.04
23	54.41
24	56.77
25	59.14
26	61.50
27	63.87
28	66.24
29	68.60
30	70.97
31	73.33
32	75.70
33	78.06
34	80.43
35	82.79
36	85.16
37	87.52
38	89.89
39	92.25
40	94.62
41	96.99
42	99.35
43	101.72
44	104.08
45	106.45
46	108.81
47	111.18
48	113.54
49	115.91
50	118.27
51	120.64
52	123.00

Employee paid at Monthly rates

Month No	Amount to subtract
1	10.25
2	20.50
3	30.75
4	41.00
5	51.25
6	61.50
7	71.75
8	82.00
9	92.25
10	102.50
11	112.75
12	123.00

Use of Table B *Example 1*

Employee's code is **404L**
The payment is made in **Week 7**

Pay in the week	£ 200	
Previous pay to date	£ 1200	
Total pay to date	£ 1400	
Less free pay in Week 7 (from Table A)	£ 545.09	
Total taxable pay to date	**£ 854.91**	

The tax is worked out by first looking in Table B on Page 6 for the nearest round figure below £854

		Tax due
It is	£ 800	£ 184.00
Look in the shaded columns for the remainder	£ 54	£ 12.42
Totals	£ 854	£ 196.42
Then give the Lower Rate Relief by looking in the table on this page for Week 7 and subtract the amount from the tax due. It is		£ 16.56
Total tax due to date		**£ 179.86**

Table C

Pages 2 and 3 tell you when to use these Tables

Employee paid at Weekly rates

Week No.	If total taxable pay to date exceeds Col 1 £	Total tax due to date Col 2 £	
1	**502**	113.10	Plus tax at 40% as shown in Table D on the amount by which the total Taxable Pay to date exceeds the figure in Col. 1
2	**1004**	226.21	
3	**1506**	339.32	
4	**2008**	452.43	
5	**2510**	565.53	
6	**3012**	678.64	
7	**3514**	791.75	
8	**4016**	904.86	
9	**4518**	1017.96	
10	**5020**	1131.07	
11	**5522**	1244.18	
12	**6024**	1357.29	
13	**6525**	1470.00	
14	**7027**	1583.10	
15	**7529**	1696.21	
16	**8031**	1809.32	
17	**8533**	1922.43	
18	**9035**	2035.53	
19	**9537**	2148.64	
20	**10039**	2261.75	
21	**10541**	2374.86	
22	**11043**	2487.96	
23	**11545**	2601.07	
24	**12047**	2714.18	
25	**12549**	2827.29	
26	**13050**	2940.00	
27	**13552**	3053.10	
28	**14054**	3166.21	
29	**14556**	3279.32	
30	**15058**	3392.43	
31	**15560**	3505.53	
32	**16062**	3618.64	
33	**16564**	3731.75	
34	**17066**	3844.86	
35	**17568**	3957.96	
36	**18070**	4071.07	
37	**18572**	4184.18	
38	**19074**	4297.29	
39	**19575**	4410.00	
40	**20077**	4523.10	
41	**20579**	4636.21	
42	**21081**	4749.32	
43	**21583**	4862.43	
44	**22085**	4975.53	
45	**22587**	5088.64	
46	**23089**	5201.75	
47	**23591**	5314.86	
48	**24093**	5427.96	
49	**24595**	5541.07	
50	**25097**	5654.18	
51	**25599**	5767.29	
52	**26100**	5880.00	

Employee paid at Monthly rates

Week No.	If total taxable pay to date exceeds Col 1 £	Total tax due to date Col 2 £	
1	**2175**	490.00	Plus tax at 40% as shown in Table D on the amount by which the total Taxable Pay to date exceeds the figure in Col. 1
2	**4350**	980.00	
3	**6525**	1470.00	
4	**8700**	1960.00	
5	**10875**	2450.00	
6	**13050**	2940.00	
7	**15225**	3430.00	
8	**17400**	3920.00	
9	**19575**	4410.00	
10	**21750**	4900.00	
11	**23925**	5390.00	
12	**26100**	5880.00	

Use of Table C *Example*

Employee's code is **404L**
The payment is made in **Week 7**

Pay in the week £ 600

Previous pay to date £ 3600

Total pay to date £ 4200

Less free pay in Week 7
(Table A) £ 545.09

Total taxable pay to date £ 3654.91

Subtract amount in Col 1
(for Week 7) £3514 tax due per Col 2
£ 791.75

Excess (£3654 - £3514) £ 140 therefore tax due per Table D = **£ 56.00**

Total tax due to date
£ 847.75

Weekly table for not contracted-out reduced rate contributions for use from 6 April 1997 to 5 April 1998

Use this table for -

- married women and widows who have the right to pay reduced rate employee's contributions for whom you hold a valid certificate CA4139, CF383 or CF38OA

Do not use this table for -

- women aged 60 or over
- women for whom you hold form CA2700, see Table C

Completing Deductions Working Sheet, form P11 or substitute -

- enter 'B' in the space provided in the 'End of Year Summary' box of form P11
- copy the figures in columns 1b and 1c of the table to columns 1b and 1c of form P11 on the line next to the tax week in which the employee is paid. You may copy the figure in column 1a of the table to column 1a of form P11 if you wish

If the exact gross pay is not shown in the table, use the next smaller figure shown.

Earnings on which employee's contributions payable 1a	Total of employee's and employer's contributions payable 1b	Employee's contributions payable 1c	▼ Employer's contributions
£	£	£	£
62	4.25	2.39	1.86
63	4.34	2.44	1.90
64	4.41	2.48	1.93
65	4.48	2.52	1.96
66	4.55	2.56	1.99
67	4.62	2.60	2.02
68	4.69	2.64	2.05
69	4.76	2.68	2.08
70	4.82	2.71	2.11
71	4.89	2.75	2.14
72	4.96	2.79	2.17
73	5.03	2.83	2.20
74	5.10	2.87	2.23
75	5.17	2.91	2.26
76	5.24	2.95	2.29
77	5.30	2.98	2.32
78	5.37	3.02	2.35
79	5.44	3.06	2.38
80	5.51	3.10	2.41
81	5.58	3.14	2.44

Earnings on which employee's contributions payable 1a	Total of employee's and employer's contributions payable 1b	Employee's contributions payable 1c	▼ Employer's contributions
£	£	£	£
82	5.65	3.18	2.47
83	5.71	3.21	2.50
84	5.78	3.25	2.53
85	5.85	3.29	2.56
86	5.92	3.33	2.59
87	5.99	3.37	2.62
88	6.06	3.41	2.65
89	6.13	3.45	2.68
90	6.19	3.48	2.71
91	6.26	3.52	2.74
92	6.33	3.56	2.77
93	6.40	3.60	2.80
94	6.47	3.64	2.83
95	6.54	3.68	2.86
96	6.61	3.72	2.89
97	6.67	3.75	2.92
98	6.74	3.79	2.95
99	6.81	3.83	2.98
100	6.88	3.87	3.01
101	6.95	3.91	3.04

▼ for information only - do not enter on Deductions Working Sheet, form P11

Table D Also to be used for Code D0

(Tax at 40%)

Income	Tax	Income	Tax	Income	Tax	Income	Tax	Income	Tax	Income	Tax
£	£	£	£	£	£	£	£	£	£	£	£
1	0.40	61	24.40	121	48.40	181	72.40	241	96.40	301	120.40
2	0.80	62	24.80	122	48.80	182	72.80	242	96.80	302	120.80
3	1.20	63	25.20	123	49.20	183	73.20	243	97.20	303	121.20
4	1.60	64	25.60	124	49.60	184	73.60	244	97.60	304	121.60
5	2.00	65	26.00	125	50.00	185	74.00	245	98.00	305	122.00
6	2.40	66	26.40	126	50.40	186	74.40	246	98.40	306	122.40
7	2.80	67	26.80	127	50.80	187	74.80	247	98.80	307	122.80
8	3.20	68	27.20	128	51.20	188	75.20	248	99.20	308	123.20
9	3.60	69	27.60	129	51.60	189	75.60	249	99.60	309	123.60
10	4.00	70	28.00	130	52.00	190	76.00	250	100.00	310	124.00
11	4.40	71	28.40	131	52.40	191	76.40	251	100.40	311	124.40
12	4.80	72	28.80	132	52.80	192	76.80	252	100.80	312	124.80
13	5.20	73	29.20	133	53.20	193	77.20	253	101.20	313	125.20
14	5.60	74	29.60	134	53.60	194	77.60	254	101.60	314	125.60
15	6.00	75	30.00	135	54.00	195	78.00	255	102.00	315	126.00
16	6.40	76	30.40	136	54.40	196	78.40	256	102.40	316	126.40
17	6.80	77	30.80	137	54.80	197	78.80	257	102.80	317	126.80
18	7.20	78	31.20	138	55.20	198	79.20	258	103.20	318	127.20
19	7.60	79	31.60	139	55.60	199	79.60	259	103.60	319	127.60
20	8.00	80	32.00	140	56.00	200	80.00	260	104.00	320	128.00
21	8.40	81	32.40	141	56.40	201	80.40	261	104.40	321	128.40
22	8.80	82	32.80	142	56.80	202	80.80	262	104.80	322	128.80
23	9.20	83	33.20	143	57.20	203	81.20	263	105.20	323	129.20
24	9.60	84	33.60	144	57.60	204	81.60	264	105.60	324	129.60
25	10.00	85	34.00	145	58.00	205	82.00	265	106.00	325	130.00
26	10.40	86	34.40	146	58.40	206	82.40	266	106.40	326	130.40
27	10.80	87	34.80	147	58.80	207	82.80	267	106.80	327	130.80
28	11.20	88	35.20	148	59.20	208	83.20	268	107.20	328	131.20
29	11.60	89	35.60	149	59.60	209	83.60	269	107.60	329	131.60
30	12.00	90	36.00	150	60.00	210	84.00	270	108.00	330	132.00
31	12.40	91	36.40	151	60.40	211	84.40	271	108.40	331	132.40
32	12.80	92	36.80	152	60.80	212	84.80	272	108.80	332	132.80
33	13.20	93	37.20	153	61.20	213	85.20	273	109.20	333	133.20
34	13.60	94	37.60	154	61.60	214	85.60	274	109.60	334	133.60
35	14.00	95	38.00	155	62.00	215	86.00	275	110.00	335	134.00
36	14.40	96	38.40	156	62.40	216	86.40	276	110.40	336	134.40
37	14.80	97	38.80	157	62.80	217	86.80	277	110.80	337	134.80
38	15.20	98	39.20	158	63.20	218	87.20	278	111.20	338	135.20
39	15.60	99	39.60	159	63.60	219	87.60	279	111.60	339	135.60
40	16.00	100	40.00	160	64.00	220	88.00	280	112.00	340	136.00
41	16.40	101	40.40	161	64.40	221	88.40	281	112.40	341	136.40
42	16.80	102	40.80	162	64.80	222	88.80	282	112.80	342	136.80
43	17.20	103	41.20	163	65.20	223	89.20	283	113.20	343	137.20
44	17.60	104	41.60	164	65.60	224	89.60	284	113.60	344	137.60
45	18.00	105	42.00	165	66.00	225	90.00	285	114.00	345	138.00
46	18.40	106	42.40	166	66.40	226	90.40	286	114.40	346	138.40
47	18.80	107	42.80	167	66.80	227	90.80	287	114.80	347	138.80
48	19.20	108	43.20	168	67.20	228	91.20	288	115.20	348	139.20
49	19.60	109	43.60	169	67.60	229	91.60	289	115.60	349	139.60
50	20.00	110	44.00	170	68.00	230	92.00	290	116.00	350	140.00
51	20.40	111	44.40	171	68.40	231	92.40	291	116.40	351	140.40
52	20.80	112	44.80	172	68.80	232	92.80	292	116.80	352	140.80
53	21.20	113	45.20	173	69.20	233	93.20	293	117.20	353	141.20
54	21.60	114	45.60	174	69.60	234	93.60	294	117.60	354	141.60
55	22.00	115	46.00	175	70.00	235	94.00	295	118.00	355	142.00
56	22.40	116	46.40	176	70.40	236	94.40	296	118.40	356	142.40
57	22.80	117	46.80	177	70.80	237	94.80	297	118.80	357	142.80
58	23.20	118	47.20	178	71.20	238	95.20	298	119.20	358	143.20
59	23.60	119	47.60	179	71.60	239	95.60	299	119.60	359	143.60
60	24.00	120	48.00	180	72.00	240	96.00	300	120.00	360	144.00

Contribution table letter

A

Monthly table

Earnings on which employee's contributions payable 1a	Total of employee's and employer's contributions payable 1b	Employee's contributions payable 1c	▼ Employer's contributions
£	£	£	**£**
1061	191.08	84.78	**106.30**
1065	191.88	85.18	**106.70**
1069	192.68	85.58	**107.10**
1073	193.48	85.98	**107.50**
1077	194.28	86.38	**107.90**
1081	195.08	86.78	**108.30**
1085	195.88	87.18	**108.70**
1089	196.68	87.58	**109.10**
1093	197.48	87.98	**109.50**
1097	198.28	88.38	**109.90**
1101	199.08	88.78	**110.30**
1105	199.88	89.18	**110.70**
1109	200.68	89.58	**111.10**
1113	201.48	89.98	**111.50**
1117	202.28	90.38	**111.90**
1121	203.08	90.78	**112.30**
1125	203.88	91.18	**112.70**
1129	204.68	91.58	**113.10**
1133	205.48	91.98	**113.50**
1137	206.28	92.38	**113.90**
1141	207.08	92.78	**114.30**
1145	207.88	93.18	**114.70**
1149	208.68	93.58	**115.10**
1153	209.48	93.98	**115.50**
1157	210.28	94.38	**115.90**
1161	211.08	94.78	**116.30**
1165	211.88	95.18	**116.70**
1169	212.68	95.58	**117.10**
1173	213.48	95.98	**117.50**
1177	214.28	96.38	**117.90**
1181	215.08	96.78	**118.30**
1185	215.88	97.18	**118.70**
1189	216.68	97.58	**119.10**
1193	217.48	97.98	**119.50**
1197	218.28	98.38	**119.90**
1201	219.08	98.78	**120.30**
1205	219.88	99.18	**120.70**
1209	220.68	99.58	**121.10**
1213	221.48	99.98	**121.50**
1217	222.28	100.38	**121.90**

Earnings on which employee's contributions payable 1a	Total of employee's and employer's contributions payable 1b	Employee's contributions payable 1c	▼ Employer's contributions
£	£	£	**£**
1221	223.08	100.78	**122.30**
1225	223.88	101.18	**122.70**
1229	224.68	101.58	**123.10**
1233	225.48	101.98	**123.50**
1237	226.28	102.38	**123.90**
1241	227.08	102.78	**124.30**
1245	227.88	103.18	**124.70**
1249	228.68	103.58	**125.10**
1253	229.48	103.98	**125.50**
1257	230.28	104.38	**125.90**
1261	231.08	104.78	**126.30**
1265	231.88	105.18	**126.70**
1269	232.68	105.58	**127.10**
1273	233.48	105.98	**127.50**
1277	234.28	106.38	**127.90**
1281	235.08	106.78	**128.30**
1285	235.88	107.18	**128.70**
1289	236.68	107.58	**129.10**
1293	237.48	107.98	**129.50**
1297	238.28	108.38	**129.90**
1301	239.08	108.78	**130.30**
1305	239.88	109.18	**130.70**
1309	240.68	109.58	**131.10**
1313	241.48	109.98	**131.50**
1317	242.28	110.38	**131.90**
1321	243.08	110.78	**132.30**
1325	243.88	111.18	**132.70**
1329	244.68	111.58	**133.10**
1333	245.48	111.98	**133.50**
1337	246.28	112.38	**133.90**
1341	247.08	112.78	**134.30**
1345	247.88	113.18	**134.70**
1349	248.68	113.58	**135.10**
1353	249.48	113.98	**135.50**
1357	250.28	114.38	**135.90**
1361	251.08	114.78	**136.30**
1365	251.88	115.18	**136.70**
1369	252.68	115.58	**137.10**
1373	253.48	115.98	**137.50**
1377	254.28	116.38	**137.90**

▼ for information only - do not enter on Deductions Working Sheet, form P11

Contribution table letter

A

Monthly table

Earnings on which employee's contributions payable 1a	Total of employee's and employer's contributions payable 1b	Employee's contributions payable 1c	▼ Employer's contributions
£	£	£	£
1381	255.08	116.78	138.30
1385	255.88	117.18	138.70
1389	256.68	117.58	139.10
1393	257.48	117.98	139.50
1397	258.28	118.38	139.90
1401	259.08	118.78	140.30
1405	259.88	119.18	140.70
1409	260.68	119.58	141.10
1413	261.48	119.98	141.50
1417	262.28	120.38	141.90
1421	263.08	120.78	142.30
1425	263.88	121.18	142.70
1429	264.68	121.58	143.10
1433	265.48	121.98	143.50
1437	266.28	122.38	143.90
1441	267.08	122.78	144.30
1445	267.88	123.18	144.70
1449	268.68	123.58	145.10
1453	269.48	123.98	145.50
1457	270.28	124.38	145.90
1461	271.08	124.78	146.30
1465	272.88	125.18	146.70
1469	272.68	125.58	147.10
1473	273.48	125.98	147.50
1477	274.28	126.38	147.90
1481	275.08	126.78	148.30
1485	275.88	127.18	148.70
1489	276.68	127.58	149.10
1493	277.48	127.98	149.50
1497	278.28	128.38	149.90
1501	279.08	128.78	150.30
1505	279.88	129.18	150.70
1509	280.68	129.58	151.10
1513	281.48	129.98	151.50
1517	282.28	130.38	151.90
1521	283.08	130.78	152.30
1525	283.88	131.18	152.70
1529	284.68	131.58	153.10
1533	285.48	131.98	153.50
1537	286.28	132.38	153.90

Earnings on which employee's contributions payable 1a	Total of employee's and employer's contributions payable 1b	Employee's contributions payable 1c	▼ Employer's contributions
£	£	£	£
1541	287.08	132.78	154.30
1545	287.88	133.18	154.70
1549	288.68	133.58	155.10
1553	289.48	133.98	155.50
1555	290.28	134.38	155.90
1561	291.08	134.78	156.30
1565	291.88	135.18	156.70
1569	292.68	135.58	157.10
1573	293.48	135.98	157.50
1577	294.28	136.38	157.90
1581	295.08	136.78	158.30
1585	295.88	137.18	158.70
1589	296.68	137.58	159.10
1593	297.48	137.98	159.50
1597	298.28	138.38	159.90
1601	299.08	138.78	160.30
1605	299.88	139.18	160.70
1609	300.68	139.58	161.10
1613	301.48	139.98	161.50
1617	302.28	140.38	161.90
1621	303.08	140.78	162.30
1625	303.88	141.18	162.70
1629	304.68	141.58	163.10
1633	305.48	141.98	163.50
1637	306.28	142.38	163.90
1641	307.08	142.78	164.30
1645	307.88	143.18	164.70
1649	308.68	143.58	165.10
1653	309.48	143.98	165.50
1657	310.28	144.38	165.90
1661	311.08	144.78	166.30
1665	311.88	145.18	166.70
1669	312.68	145.58	167.10
1673	313.48	145.98	167.50
1677	314.28	146.38	167.90
1681	315.08	146.78	168.30
1685	315.88	147.18	168.70
1689	316.68	147.58	169.10
1693	317.48	147.98	169.50
1697	318.28	148.38	169.90

▼ for information only - do not enter on Deductions Working Sheet, form P11

Weekly table for not contracted-out employer only contributions for use from 6 April 1997 to 5 April 1998

Use this table for -

- employees who are State pension age or over, for whom you hold a valid certificate CA4140 or CF384
- women for whom you hold a valid certificate CA2700

Completing Deductions Working Sheet, form P11 or substitute -

- enter 'C' in the space provided in the 'End of Year Summary' box of form P11
- copy the figures in column 1b of the table to column 1b of form P11 on the line next to the tax week in which the employee is paid. You may copy the figure in column 1a of the table to column 1a of form P11 if you wish

If the exact gross pay is not shown in the table, use the next smaller figure shown.

Earnings on which contributions payable 1a	Total of employer's contributions payable 1b	Earnings on which contributions payable 1a	Total of employer's contributions payable 1b
£	£	£	£
62	1.86	82	2.47
63	1.90	83	2.50
64	1.93	84	2.53
65	1.96	85	2.56
66	1.99	86	2.59
67	2.02	87	2.62
68	2.05	88	2.65
69	2.08	89	2.68
70	2.11	90	2.71
71	2.14	91	2.74
72	2.17	92	2.77
73	2.20	93	2.80
74	2.23	94	2.83
75	2.26	95	2.86
76	2.29	96	2.89
77	2.32	97	2.92
78	2.35	98	2.95
79	2.38	99	2.98
80	2.41	100	3.01
81	2.44	101	3.04

Earnings on which contributions payable 1a	Total of employer's contributions payable 1b	Earnings on which contributions payable 1a	Total of employer's contributions payable 1b
£	£	£	£
102	3.07	122	6.12
103	3.10	123	6.17
104	3.13	124	6.22
105	3.16	125	6.27
106	3.19	126	6.32
107	3.22	127	6.37
108	3.25	128	6.42
109	3.28	129	6.47
110	5.52	130	6.52
111	5.57	131	6.57
112	5.62	132	6.62
113	5.67	133	6.67
114	5.72	134	6.72
115	5.77	135	6.77
116	5.82	136	6.82
117	5.87	137	6.87
118	5.92	138	6.92
119	5.97	139	6.97
120	6.02	140	7.02
121	6.07	141	7.07

Statutory Sick Pay daily rates table

How to use the Statutory Sick Pay daily rates table

The daily rate of Statutory Sick Pay is the weekly rate of Statutory Sick Pay divided by the number of qualifying days (QDs) in the week, beginning Sunday, for which you are paying Statutory Sick Pay. In the following example, Sunday is not a qualifying day, so you cannot pay Statutory Sick Pay for that day.

Example
An employee has average weekly earnings of £100.
The qualifying days in the week for which you are paying Statutory Sick Pay are Monday to Friday.
Your employee is sick from Sunday to Friday.
No waiting days have yet been served.

Calculation
The average weekly earning are more than the lower earning limit, £62, so Statutory Sick Pay is payable if all the other qualifying conditions are also satisfied.

The first three qualifying days are waiting days. Statutory Sick Pay is not payable for those days so you must only pay Statutory Sick Pay for Thursday and Friday in this week.

There are five qualifying days in the week so now find '5' in the 'Number of QDs in week' column.

You have to pay Statutory Sick Pay for two days so move across now to the column headed by '2'. This gives the amount, '£22.28', of Statutory Sick Pay you must pay. Remember, Statutory Sick Pay is subject ot PAYE and National Insurance deductions.

Statutory Sick Pay Daily Rates Table

Unrounded daily rates £	No of QDs in week	1 £	2 £	3 £	4 £	5 £	6 £	7 £
7.9571	7	7.96	15.92	23.88	31.83	39.79	47.75	55.70
9.2833	6	9.29	18.57	27.85	37.14	46.42	55.70	
11.1400	5	11.14	22.28	33.42	44.56	55.70		
13.9250	4	13.93	27.85	41.78	55.70			
18.5667	3	18.57	37.14	55.70				
27.8500	2	27.85	55.70					
54.7000	1	55.70						

Unrounded rates are included for employers with computerised payroll systems

Statutory Maternity Pay Tables

COLUMN 1 Expected week of confinement (EWC) (see note 1)	COLUMN 2 Qualifying week (QW) commencing Sunday (see note 2)	COLUMN 3 Latest start date for 26 weeks employment (see note 3)	COLUMN 4 11th week before the EWC (see note 4)	COLUMN 5 6th week before the EWC (see note 5)
30 11 97 to 06 12 97	17 08 97	01 03 97	14 09 97	19 10 97
07 12 97 to 13 12 97	24 08 97	08 03 97	21 09 97	26 10 97
14 12 97 to 20 12 97	31 08 97	15 03 97	28 09 97	02 11 97
21 12 97 to 27 12 97	07 09 97	22 03 97	05 10 97	09 11 97
28 12 97 to 03 01 98	14 09 97	29 03 97	12 10 97	16 11 97
04 01 98 to 10 01 98	21 09 97	05 04 97	19 10 97	23 11 97
11 01 98 to 17 01 98	28 09 97	12 04 97	26 10 97	30 11 97
18 01 98 to 24 01 98	05 10 97	19 04 97	01 11 97	07 12 97
25 01 98 to 31 01 98	12 10 97	26 04 97	08 11 97	14 12 97
01 02 98 to 07 02 98	19 10 97	03 05 97	16 11 97	21 12 97
08 02 98 to 14 02 98	26 10 97	10 05 97	23 11 97	28 12 97
15 02 98 to 21 02 98	02 11 97	17 05 97	30 11 97	04 01 98
22 02 98 to 28 02 98	09 11 97	24 05 97	07 12 97	11 01 98
01 03 98 to 07 03 98	16 11 97	31 05 97	14 12 97	18 01 98
08 03 98 to 14 03 98	23 11 97	07 06 97	21 12 97	25 01 98
15 03 98 to 21 03 98	30 11 97	14 06 97	28 12 97	01 02 98
22 03 98 to 28 03 98	07 12 97	21 06 97	04 01 98	08 02 98
29 03 98 to 04 04 98	14 12 97	28 06 97	11 01 98	15 02 98
05 04 98 to 11 04 98	21 12 97	05 07 97	18 01 98	22 02 98
12 04 98 to 18 04 98	28 12 97	12 07 97	25 01 98	01 03 98
19 04 98 to 25 04 98	04 01 98	19 07 97	01 02 98	08 03 98
26 04 98 to 02 05 98	11 01 98	26 07 97	08 02 98	15 03 98
03 05 98 to 09 05 98	18 01 98	02 08 97	15 02 98	22 03 98
10 05 98 to 16 05 98	25 01 98	09 08 97	22 02 98	29 03 98
17 05 98 to 23 05 98	01 02 98	16 08 97	01 03 98	05 04 98
24 05 98 to 30 05 98	08 02 98	23 08 97	08 03 98	12 04 98
31 05 98 to 06 06 98	15 02 98	30 08 97	15 03 98	19 04 98
07 06 98 to 13 06 98	22 02 98	06 09 97	22 03 98	26 04 98
14 06 98 to 20 06 98	01 03 98	13 09 97	29 03 98	03 05 98
21 06 98 to 27 06 98	08 03 98	20 09 97	05 04 98	10 05 98
28 06 98 to 04 07 98	15 03 98	27 09 97	12 04 98	17 05 98
05 07 98 to 11 06 98	22 03 98	04 10 97	19 04 98	24 05 98
12 07 98 to 18 07 98	29 03 98	11 10 97	26 04 98	31 05 98
19 07 98 to 25 07 98	05 04 98	18 10 97	03 05 98	07 06 98
26 07 98 to 01 08 98	12 04 98	25 10 97	10 05 98	14 06 98

Appendix 3

Answers to Exercises

Exercise 1 (Page 44)

Month no	Week no	Pay in the week or month including Statutory Sick Pay/Statutory Maternity Pay 2 £	Total pay to date 3 £	Total free pay to date (Table A) 4a £	K codes only: Total 'additional pay' to date (Table A) 4b £	Total taxable pay to date i.e. column 3 *minus* column 4a **or** column 3 *plus* column 4b 5 £	Total tax due to date as shown by Taxable Pay Tables 6 £	K codes only: Tax due at end of current period Mark refunds 'R' 6a £	K codes only: Regulatory limit i.e. 50% of column 2 entry 6b £	Tax deducted or refunded in the week or month. Mark refunds 'R' 7 £	K codes only: Tax not deducted owing to the Regulatory limit 8 £	For employer's use
	1											
	2											
	3											
1	4	1100 00	1100 00	437 42		662 58	142 01			142 01		
	5											
	6											
	7											
2	8	1200 00	2300 00	874 84		1425 16	307 25			165 24		
	9											
	10											
	11											
	12											
3	13	1400 00	3700 00	1312 26		2387 74	518 26			211 01		
	14											
	15											
	16											
4	17	1250 00	4950 00	1749 68		3200 32	695 00			176 74		
	18											
	19											
	20											
5	21	1500 00	6450 00	2187 10		4262 90	929 01			234 01		
	22											
	23											
	24											
	25											
6	26											
	27											
	28											
	29											
7	30											

Exercise 2 (Page 71)

Month no	Week no	Pay in the week or month including Statutory Sick Pay/Statutory Maternity Pay 2 £	Total pay to date 3 £	Total free pay to date (Table A) 4a £	K codes only: Total 'additional pay' to date (Table A) 4b £	Total taxable pay to date i.e. column 3 *minus* column 4a **or** column 3 *plus* column 4b 5 £	Total tax due to date as shown by Taxable Pay Tables 6 £	K codes only: Tax due at end of current period Mark refunds 'R' 6a £	K codes only: Regulatory limit i.e. 50% of column 2 entry 6b £	Tax deducted or refunded in the week or month. Mark refunds 'R' 7 £	K codes only: Tax not deducted owing to the Regulatory limit 8 £	For employer's use
	1											
	2											
	3											
1	4	1100 00	1100 00		355 75	1455 75	324 40	324 40	550 00	324 40		
	5											
	6											
	7											
2	8	1200 00	2300 00		711 50	3011 50	672 03	347 63	600 00	347 63		
	9											
	10											
	11											
	12											
3	13	1400 00	3700 00		1067 25	4767 25	1065 66	393 63	700 00	393 63		
	14											
	15											
	16											
4	17	1250 00	4950 00		1423 00	6373 00	1424 79	359 13	625 00	359 13		
	18											
	19											
	20											
5	21	1500 00	6450 00		1778 75	8228 75	1841 19	416 40	750 00	416 40		
	22											
	23											
	24											
	25											
6	26											
	27											
	28											
	29											
7	30											

Exercise 3 (Page 140)

Earnings recorded in column 1a should not exceed the Upper Earnings Limit

For employer's use	Earnings on which employee's contributions payable *Whole pounds only* 1a £	Total of employee's and employer's contributions payable 1b £	Employee's contributions payable 1c £	Earnings on which employee's contributions at contracted-out rate payable included in col 1a *Whole pounds only* 1d £	Employee's contributions at contracted-out rate included in column 1c 1e £	Statutory Sick Pay in the week or month included in column 2 1f £	Statutory Maternity Pay in the week or month included in column 2 1g £	Statutory Maternity Pay recovered 1h £	Month no	Week no
										1
										2
										3
	1100	198 28	88 38						1	4
										5
										6
										7
	1200	218 28	98 38						2	8
										9
										10
										11
										12
	1400	258 28	118 38						3	13
										14
										15
										16
	1250	228 68	103 58						4	17
										18
										19
										20
	1500	278 28	128 38						5	21
										22
										23
										24
										25
									6	26
										27
										28
										29
									7	30
	Total c/fwd	Total c/fwd	Total c/fwd	Total c/fwd	Total c/fwd	Total c/fwd	Total c/fwd	Total c/fwd		

Exercise 4 (Page 148)

	£
Car Benefit 11250 x 35%	3937
Less Discount for high mileage 2/3	(2625)
	1312
Less Discount for age 1/3	(437)
	875
Add Fuel Benefit	1010
Total Benefit	1885

Tax payable £1885 @ 10% = £188.50

Exercise 5 (Page 157)

Employee	**Average Weekly Earnings £**	**No of Qualifying Days in Week**	**Days Sick**	**SSP Payable in Week £**
Jan	220	6	Sunday to Friday	£27.85
Joe	199	5	Sunday to Sunday	£22.28
Stuart	56	5	Tuesday to Friday	Nil
Donna	136	4	Monday to Wednesday	Nil

Appendix 4

Miscellaneous Payroll Deductions

Several payroll deductions do not fit neatly into any particular section of the book. These have been reproduced here for completeness.

Approved 'Save As You Earn' Share Option Schemes

Companies can set up a Save As You Earn (SAYE) share scheme. This allows employees to purchase shares in the company on favourable terms.

In order to participate in the scheme, employees must enter into a contract to save a fixed amount every month for a fixed period of time. Employers are allowed to contribute as much as they want, subject to a minimum monthly contribution of £5 and a maximum monthly contribution of £250. The duration of the scheme can be for three, five or seven years. Under normal circumstances, the employer will deduct money from the employee's salary which is paid directly into a bank or building society. All employees must be treated under the same rules. However, some employees may be allowed to buy more shares than others depending on criteria like length of service, level of pay etc.

The scheme is attractive because employees are allowed to buy shares at a fixed price which can be as low as 80% of the current market price. If the shares fall in value over the savings period, the employee is not contractually bound to take up the option, he may withdraw the savings and spend the money in some other way.

There is no relief for PAYE on amounts deducted under the Save As You Earn scheme, however there are several other tax advantages. For example, the employee:

- is not taxed when he receives the share option
- is not normally taxed when he uses the proceeds of the scheme to buy shares
- can transfer the shares into a single company Personal Equity Plan where the proceeds can accumulate free of income tax and capital gains tax.

At the end of the savings contract, the saver is entitled to a tax free bonus as follows:

- The 3 year savings contract attracts a bonus equal to 3 monthly contributions
- The 5 year savings contract attracts a bonus equal to 9 monthly contributions
- The 7 year savings contract attracts a bonus equal to 18 monthly contributions.

There are additional conditions and restrictions applying to the scheme. Details can be found in the following Inland Revenue leaflets.

IR97 Approved Save As You Earn share option schemes - an outline for employees (available from local tax offices)

IR98 Approved SAYE share option schemes - explanatory notes
(available from The Public Enquiry Room, Inland Revenue, Room G1, West Wing, Somerset House, Strand, London, WC2R 1LB, telephone 0171 438 6420).

Payroll Giving

Payroll giving is a scheme which enables an employee to contribute to a charity free of income tax. Like all tax savings scheme, there are restrictions to prevent abuse. In a nutshell, the scheme operates as follows:

- An employee authorises his employer to make deductions from his wage or salary. The maximum contribution to charity is £1200 in any tax year. The employer deducts income tax from the employee's earnings *after* the gift has been deducted. This provides relief at the employee's top rate of tax.

- The employer collects the donations and forwards them to an Approved Agency for the payroll giving scheme. A list of approved agencies is available from the Inland Revenue Financial Intermediaries and Claims Office, telephone 051-472-6000. At the time of writing, there were more than 11 charitable agencies which accept donations from the business community.

- Donations are sent to charitable agencies each month at the same time as the employer sends his PAYE remittance to the Collector of Taxes. The charity will provide a receipt for the donations.

- There is no obligation for an employer to run a payroll giving scheme. The costs of running the scheme have to be borne by the employer; however, the costs are allowable as a deduction aganst business profits.

- The Inland Revenue requires the employer to keep records. These are:

  - A copy of the contract with the agency
  - A copy of your employee's authority to make deductions
  - Details of each payment made by each employee
  - Receipts from the agency charity.

The following Inland Revenue leaflets give details of the payroll giving scheme:

Payroll Giving Scheme - A guide for employees
Payroll Giving Scheme - A guide for employers.

(Neither of these leaflets has an Inland Revenue reference number).

Attachment of Earnings

Courts have the power to force employers to make deductions from employees' wages. The deductions are then paid to the Court.

The circumstances surrounding the court order are of no consequence to the payroll department; however, the edict has to be complied with. Ensure that 'attachments of earnings' are made from *net* pay (ie after deduction of PAYE and NI) otherwise the relief would wrongly be given on earnings to which no tax relief should apply.